Edited by Naomi Starkey   May–August 2004

7	**Psalm 139** Stephen Rand	1–8 May
15	**Heaven and hell** Veronica Zundel	9–22 May
30	**Romans 8** David Spriggs	23 May–5 June
45	**Power and authority** John Proctor	6–19 June
60	**Ephesians 3:1—4:16** Margaret Silf	20 June–3 July
74	**Hebrews 8—10** Adrian Plass	4–17 July
89	**Luke's miracles** Jane Cornish	18–31 July
104	**Bible places** David Winter	1–14 August
119	**Luke's parables** Jenny Robertson	15–31 August
137	The New Daylight Magazine	

Suggestions for using *New Daylight*

Find a regular time and place, if possible, where you can read and pray undisturbed. Before you begin, take time to be still and perhaps use the BRF prayer. Then read the Bible passage slowly (try reading it aloud if you find it over-familiar), followed by the comment. You can also use *New Daylight* for group study and discussion, if you prefer.

The prayer or point for reflection can be a starting point for your own meditation and prayer. Many people like to keep a journal to record their thoughts about a Bible passage and items for prayer. In *New Daylight* we also note the Sundays and special festivals from the Church calendar, to keep in step with the Christian year.

New Daylight and the Bible

New Daylight contributors use a range of Bible versions, and you will find a list of the versions used in each issue at the back of the notes on page 154. You are welcome to use your own preferred version alongside the passage printed in the notes, and this can be particularly helpful if the Bible text has been abridged.

New Daylight affirms that the whole of the Bible is God's revelation to us, and we should read, reflect on and learn from every part of both Old and New Testaments. Usually the printed comment presents a straight-forward 'thought for the day', but sometimes it may also raise questions rather than simply providing answers, as we wrestle with some of the more difficult passages of Scripture.

Writers in this issue

Stephen Rand is Prayer and Campaigns Director for Tearfund, co-chair of Jubilee Debt Campaign and author of *Guinea Pig for Lunch* (Hodder, 1998), which tells stories from his travels around the world with Tearfund.

Veronica Zundel is an Oxford graduate, writer and journalist. She lives with her husband and young son in North London, where they belong to the Mennonite Church.

David Spriggs is a Baptist minister, currently working as Head of Church Relations for Bible Society, where he had also been Project Director for The Open Book.

John Proctor is married to Elaine with two adult children. He works for the United Reformed Church, teaching the New Testament to students in Cambridge. Before that he was a parish minister in Glasgow. John has written *The People's Bible Commentary: Matthew* (BRF, 2001) and *Urban God* (BRF, 2002).

Margaret Silf is an ecumenical Christian, committed to working across and beyond the denominational divides. For most of her working life she was employed in the computer industry, but left paid employment to devote herself to writing and accompanying others on their spiritual journey.

Adrian Plass is an internationally popular writer and speaker in many countries. His most recent book for BRF is *When You Walk*.

Jane Cornish is the 2000 winner of the Shelagh Brown Memorial Prize. She has been writing group study notes for many years for her local Anglican church and is now training for local lay ministry.

David Winter is retired from parish ministry. An honorary Canon of Christ Church, Oxford, he is well known as a writer and broadcaster.

Jenny Robertson lived for a number of years in Russia, working alongside her husband in St Petersburg. She has written many books for both adults and children, including *Strength of the Hills* for BRF. She has also had a number of books of poetry published.

Further BRF reading for this issue

For more in-depth coverage of some of the passages in these
Bible reading notes, we recommend the following titles:

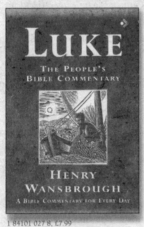

1 84101 027 8, £7.99

1 84101 047 2, £7.99

1 84101 119 3, £7.99

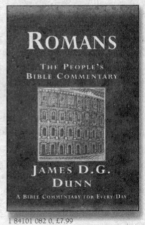

1 84101 082 0, £7.99

Naomi Starkey writes...

This May to August copy of *New Daylight* is the one that (all being well) accompanies readers off on their holidays. Perhaps the little book is stuffed into the side pocket of a battered rucksack, slipped into the glove compartment of the family car or even carefully conveyed in a plastic wallet in a piece of designer hand luggage (depending on the kind of traveller you are).

Echoing this theme, David Winter has written notes for the first part of August entitled 'Bible Places', looking at some of the locations identified in the Bible, especially those that might be sites of modern-day pilgrimage. As he says in his introduction, 'Places are important to us: our place of birth, our home town, sites we have visited on holiday or pilgrimage, the burial places of relatives and friends... Places are also important in God's story... Eden, Ararat, Ur of the Chaldees, Sinai, Canaan, Jordan, Bethlehem, Jerusalem. It would be no exaggeration to say that the history of our faith is largely the history of people... and places.'

If you are planning a trip to the Middle East, or, closer to home, if you find yourself stopping for a tea break in a village with a 19th-century chapel named Bethel, Peniel, or Zion, these notes will have special relevance to you!

I would also like to introduce you to three more contributors who have joined the *New Daylight* writing team—although one of them has already made a guest appearance a couple of years ago.

John Proctor, who has written two weeks on scriptural perspectives on power and authority, teaches New Testament to students in Cambridge and works for the United Reformed Church. He has written two books for BRF—*Urban God* (2002) and the volume on Matthew in our *People's Bible Commentary* series (2001).

Stephen Rand, who brings us a series of reflections on Psalm 139, is Prayer and Campaigns Director for Tearfund, co-chair of Jubilee Debt Campaign and author of *Guinea Pig for Lunch* (Hodder, 1998), which tells stories from his travels around the world with Tearfund.

And rejoining the team after a previous 'guest appearance' is Jane Cornish, winner of the Shelagh Brown Memorial Prize (it was her prize-winning notes that appeared in the January–April 2002 issue). Jane is training for lay ministry in the Anglican Church.

The BRF Prayer

Almighty God,
you have taught us that your word is a lamp for
our feet and a light for our path. Help us, and
all who prayerfully read your word, to deepen
our fellowship with each other through your
love. And in so doing may we come to know
you more fully, love you more truly, and follow
more faithfully in the steps of your son Jesus
Christ, who lives and reigns with you and the
Holy Spirit, one God for evermore. Amen.

You know

O Lord, you have searched me and you know me. You know when I sit and when I rise; you perceive my thoughts from afar. You discern my going out and my lying down; you are familiar with all my ways. Before a word is on my tongue you know it completely, O Lord.

George Orwell's novel *1984* captured one of the major sources of personal unease in modern society in the disturbing, all-pervasive but unseen and unknown figure of Big Brother. Whatever you did, wherever you went, whoever you met—he was there. Big Brother was watching you.

Now, of course, we watch *Big Brother*. Our worst fear has been turned into trivial entertainment, because we are on the outside, observing the victims. Constantly under surveillance, some can't take it and break down under the pressure.

The psalmist knows how this feels. He describes a God who needs no CCTV cameras to keep us under scrutiny. Indeed, he is not limited to what he can see from the outside. He can—and does—know us from the inside. Our brain patterns are as clear as a printout; our words are heard even before they reach the tip of our tongue. Our whole beings have gone through the scanner, and the results are plain to see. This is complete knowledge. It is comprehensive. It is awesome. He knows us better than we know ourselves.

It is worth allowing time to let this sink in. We live our lives fondly imagining we are in control of what people know about us. Before almighty God, though, we are stripped bare. I still remember the day that this realization hit me; the moment when a theological truth became an emotional reality. I recognized in that moment the depth of the gulf between myself and a holy God. The tears flowed… and slowly a new depth emerged. That this is a God who knows the worst about us—and loves us just the same. Jesus did not die just for nice people, even good people. He died for sinners, in the full knowledge of every detail of their sin. That is even more awesome.

Prayer

Thank you, holy God, for the deep reassurance that comes from knowing that even when you know us so well you love us so much.

SR

Your hand upon me

You hem me in—behind and before; you have laid your hand upon me. Such knowledge is too wonderful for me, too lofty for me to attain.

A high tower can be a prison or a place of safety. You can be hemmed in and either feel restricted or secure. A hand on the shoulder could belong to an arresting police officer or your closest friend. Different people will read these simple verses and have wildly differing reactions. Many will recognize that their experience of God has included both extremes. God has needed to arrest some in order to become their friend.

David reflects that not only does God know him inside out, but, having given him the most thorough examination, has decided to touch him. God's knowledge of him was not dispassionate observation or even curious scrutiny; it was the basis of an intimate personal relationship. No wonder it was too wonderful for him to grasp fully.

As children, some of us lined up in the playground when the teams were being picked, desperate to catch the captain's eye, longing to be chosen. For others, the words 'I want two or three of you to come out to the front' were sufficient to strike dread into the heart and a deep desire for invisibility to descend.

God intends us to know that when he lays his hand on us, it is not a passing whim or a divine version of the fickle finger of fate. God knows us, and he chooses us. He chooses us by touching us—and some of us know the kind of joy those with leprosy experienced who discovered they were not considered unclean by Jesus.

Best of all, God lays his hand on us because he is choosing us to play a part in his plan and purpose for his creation. When he laid his hand on David, it was to make him a king, part of the family tree of Jesus. When God lays his hand on us, we too become part of the same family tree, children of the King of kings.

Sundy reflection

When we join in worship, we open ourselves once again to the touch of God on our lives—assuring us of his acceptance, prompting us to praise and revealing his purpose for us as part of his worldwide Church.

SR

No escape

Where can I go from your Spirit? Where can I flee from your presence? If I go up to the heavens, you are there; if I make my bed in the depths, you are there. If I rise on the wings of the dawn, if I settle on the far side of the sea, even there your hand will guide me, your right hand will hold me fast. If I say, 'Surely the darkness will hide me and the light become night around me,' even the darkness will not be dark to you; the night will shine like the day, for darkness is as light to you.

I loved geography at school. I have loved it even more as my work at the Tearfund has turned it from abstract classroom knowledge into technicolour reality. It has been a privilege to head up the river Patuca into the Honduran rainforest in a dugout canoe; it was great to watch the parakeets roosting in the grapefruit trees as the sun set over the Paraguayan Chaco. Best of all, though, is discovering the truth of these verses. When I shared a simple communion in a ramshackle church in a shantytown in Lima, Peru, I was reminded that God is there in person and God is there in people.

The presence of God is more than a universal geographical reality. The 'heavens' and the 'depths' remind us that it is a spiritual reality, too. Astronauts and deep-sea explorers may be most aware and most grateful for the presence of God; but each one of us can be reassured that in our own highs or lows God is there.

The dimensions filled by God's presence keep tumbling out: he is there in all time and for all time; no physical barrier, even one as vast and powerful as the sea, can keep him away. The creator of the sun and moon is not restricted by day or night, light or darkness.

What is the purpose of God's all-encompassing presence? Not to hassle or hustle us, but to guide and reassure.

Prayer

Loving Father, today, wherever I go, whatever I do, grant me the knowledge of your presence, the reassurance of your guiding hand and the security of your loving grip.

SR

Fearfully and wonderfully made

For you created my inmost being; you knit me together in my mother's womb. I praise you because I am fearfully and wonderfully made; your works are wonderful, I know that full well. My frame was not hidden from you when I was made in the secret place. When I was woven together in the depths of the earth, your eyes saw my unformed body...

Babies are wonderful—so many mothers have told me that I know it to be true. I'm not too good at making those cooing noises over the pram; I'm only a little better at the cuddling and moderately fazed by a damp nappy. I am a man, after all. I'm also a dad. Katharine emerged after two days of labour in the middle of a heat wave; three years later Helen arrived and precipitated a minor medical emergency. When I held them in my arms for the first time, there was awe and wonder, delight and deep joy.

If I have had the privilege of that experience, then how much more has our Father God? David takes his exploration of the presence of God into a new dimension, revealing to us that God's knowledge of us began as we began; his interaction with us started when we were incapable of response. Nor did we roll off a divine conveyor belt at the end of a soulless production line. Each of us is a carefully and personally fashioned individual.

So we marvel at the tiny fingers and tiny toes. The intricacies of human anatomy never cease to fascinate or amaze. David goes deeper. Human beings are not just a masterful creation of muscle and bone, sinew and tissue. Each of us has personality. Each of us is made in the image of God. The all-powerful, all-knowing being bothered himself with our inmost being. The creator of the universe took a personal interest in our creation. When we were 'knit together', he may have followed a pattern, but each of us is unique: we come with a hand-made designer label.

Prayer

Almighty God, revealed as a loving Father, thank you that you poured your creativity into me. Thank you for physical life; thank you for the work of your Holy Spirit in giving new life and creating the possibility of me becoming the kind of person you always intended me to be.

SR

Ordained

All the days ordained for me were written in your book before one of them came to be.

This psalm is full of thoughts and revelations about God that have the capacity to scare and reassure us in almost equal measure.

David now enters the celestial library—a vast collection of beautifully bound volumes. The name of the author is the same on each one: Father God. Each is a biography, each one unique, simply bearing the name of the subject. Some seem well-used and often-read; others are in mint condition, waiting to be opened for the first time. Some are thinner volumes than others. Each is complete.

Here again is the God many who don't know him find threatening and difficult. All our days known before we start? Our lives spent hurtling towards a tombstone that already carries the date? Are we not allowed any room for manoeuvre? No court of appeal? It's a reminder of that wonderful film *A Matter of Life and Death*, with David Niven mistakenly harvested by the grim reaper and pleading at the gates of heaven to be allowed to return and complete his allotted time on earth. It's a recurring Hollywood theme because it touches the raw nerve of our mortality.

That's why I love the word 'ordained' in this passage. Yes, it can mean fated or predetermined, but it can also mean appointed. These are not just days in the calendar that pass by relentlessly, with the clock ticking remorselessly onwards. These are days that God has given to us, made for us. They are ours for us to use in his service, for our enjoyment. I'll leave God as the one knowing the total number and I'll concentrate on making the most of each one.

God's appointment diary has our name on every day because God has chosen to meet us; he wants to meet us and longs for us to turn up each day, every day.

Prayer and praise

Day by day, dear Lord of you
Three things I pray:
To see you more clearly,
To love you more dearly,
To follow you more nearly,
Day by day.

St Richard of Chichester

'This is the day that the Lord has made; let us rejoice and be glad in it' (Psalm 118:24, NRSV).

SR

Precious thoughts

How precious to me are your thoughts, O God! How vast is the sum of them! Were I to count them, they would outnumber the grains of sand. When I awake, I am still with you.

When I first became aware of computers, they were vast calculating machines, needing their own rooms, carefully protected with air filters and security locks. As time has passed, they have become smaller and smaller, more and more powerful. The more amazing they get, the less we are amazed because we have become so used to being amazed.

David was amazed by his thoughts about God's thoughts. When he thought about the thinking that God must do, his brain began to hurt. Perhaps he was sitting by himself in a desert place, watching the sand dunes shimmer off into infinity while the grains of sand ran through his fingers. After all, if God knew all his thoughts, then he knew everyone else's thoughts; at the same time God's thinking was maintaining the whole universe and guiding each of his people.

It is not just that God is so much greater than even the greatest computer, nor even that the greatest computer could not count God's thoughts any more than David could. What makes David really want to break into praise is that God's thoughts are precious to him. Why? Because in all their vast number, there is still space for David. When he sleeps, God does not; his thoughts continue to sustain and care for David. Then he wakes and his first realization is that he is still in God's thoughts. No wonder he feels that these are precious thoughts.

I once met an African Christian whose first thought on waking was to thank God for having brought him safely to another day. My first thought is more likely to be 'What day of the week is it?' Perhaps I should practise starting the day by lining up my thoughts with God's thoughts. He's thinking about me; he's starting the day with me. That's precious.

Reflection

The alarm rings. Your eyes open. Propped against the clock is an envelope. It wasn't there when you switched off the light. You open the envelope and a beautifully simple card that just says 'Thinking of you.' Inside it is signed 'God'.

SR

Enemies

If only you would slay the wicked, O God! Away from me, you blood-thirsty men! They speak of you with evil intent; your adversaries misuse your name. Do I not hate those who hate you, O Lord, and abhor those who rise up against you? I have nothing but hatred for them; I count them my enemies.

Yesterday, we reflected on the preciousness of God's thoughts. Today, we have 'slay the wicked'. Same person, same psalm—and same God. That's why it is particularly important to sense the source of David's vehemence.

There's lots of anger about in our society. Take road rage, for example. I always remember when I'm travelling to preach at a church to drive particularly graciously as it's so embarrassing to recognize the person in the front row as the one you earlier decided to help understand why driving steadily in the middle lane is such a bad idea.

More seriously, there are fellow Christians who have every reason to hate the wicked. My wife stood at Heathrow Airport holding a sign saying 'Isaiah'. She was not searching for an ancient prophet, but a Sudanese pastor who has seen his family murdered in a civil war and wants God's help to love his enemies because that is what Jesus demands of his followers.

What has made David angry? People who hate God, who misuse his name. David is offended on behalf of the one whose thoughts are so precious. We can be quick to defend ourselves, slow to defend others. We can be upset when someone abuses us, far less concerned on God's account.

This is not about rebuking people who swear. It is about being genuinely hurt when God's name is abused by those who claim to kill in his name. God has many enemies and some of them bear the name 'Christian'. It is about raising our voice when God's values are denied and rubbished and standing up for the rights of others rather than our own. In making sure that we hate what God hates, it is wise to remember that God will arise to scatter his enemies in his own way and in his own time.

Prayer

May God bless you with anger…
at injustice, oppression, and exploitation of people, so that you may work for justice, freedom and peace.

Extract from a Franciscan benediction

SR

Search me, lead me

Search me, O God, and know my heart; test me and know my anxious thoughts. See if there is any offensive way in me, and lead me in the way everlasting.

The psalm begins with the recognition that God has searched the psalmist and known him. It ends with a prayer that this process would continue. This request can only come from one who is humble before the greatness and holiness of God. He has explored the completeness and fullness of God's knowledge of him—in geographical location, in psychological totality, in physical entirety and in all aspects of time.

He has acknowledged that he cannot escape from God. He has embraced God's presence for its life-giving security and life-enhancing fullness. It is on the basis of this experience and this commitment that he is willing to submit once again to God's scrutiny. His fear is of losing God rather than of losing face. He knows he cannot hide from God, and cannot hide his sin from him; he also knows that God can find him and love him, and deal with the sin in a way that he can't.

The journey of life that began in his mother's womb carries the promise of eternity. The way everlasting is not the frustration of always travelling and never arriving.

It is the assurance of being taken by the hand of a loving Father who will never let you go, and lead you into life beyond anything we can imagine. Here is the same paradox that Jesus explained as 'Whoever finds his life will lose it, and whoever loses his life for my sake will find it' (Matthew 10:39). It is only when we embrace God's total knowledge of us that we can be set free to begin the journey to total awareness of God.

The apostle Paul put it like this: 'Now we see but a poor reflection as in a mirror; then we shall see face to face. Now I know in part; then I shall know fully, even as I am fully known' (1 Corinthians 13:12).

Prayer

Why not pause, and use today's verses as a prayer: 'Search me, O God, and know my heart; test me and know my anxious thoughts. See if there is any offensive way in me, and lead me in the way everlasting.'

SR

Heaven and hell

Hanging washing on the line the other day, I came up with my own image of hell: matching socks for eternity, and always having one left over! Heaven is the Greenbelt festival (with more toilets and no rain), where I meet up with all my old friends.

No doubt you have your own pictures of what might lie beyond death. The Bible gives us remarkably little information, so Christians have been free to exercise their imaginations. They have done so extensively, coming up with limbo, purgatory, fallen angels and all sorts of other theories.

In reaction to this, my husband's Christadelphian forebears decided to do away with demons in red tights with pitchforks and angels in white nighties and take a hard look at what the Bible actually does say. I think they were right in this and I have attempted to do the same in these notes.

I was surprised to find while reading how much Jesus says about judgment, hell and destruction—'gentle Jesus meek and mild' doesn't seem to fit here! I also noticed that he gives little in the way of details about an afterlife, either positive or negative. Instead he talks a great deal about God's kingdom, often using the image of a huge party.

Some evangelists love to threaten hell and promise heaven as part of their emotional armoury to get people to listen to Jesus. We've all heard 'fire and brimstone' preaching or seen tracts saying 'Are you sure you'll get to heaven?' It's notable that the early Church didn't mention either hell or heaven in its preaching (see Peter's sermon in Acts 2, for example). They were keener on telling the good news that, in Jesus, God's kingdom has come close and you can just walk into it.

It seems, then, that we shouldn't be so interested in where we or others are going after death that we forget to live the Jesus life here on earth. Nor should we indulge in condemning others to hell. Jesus never said that we would be the judges of good and evil, but that 'on the last day the word that I have spoken will serve as judge' (John 12:48, NRSV).

It is important, though, that we speak that word and obey it faithfully. A vision of God's ultimate transformation of this world, and the destruction of evil, should help motivate us to do that. There is justice in the end. Our work is not in vain (1 Corinthians 15:58).

Veronica Zundel

Is that all?

For I know that my Redeemer lives, and that at the last he will stand upon the earth; and after my skin has been thus destroyed, then in my flesh I shall see God.

Where can I go from your spirit? Or where can I flee from your presence? If I ascend to heaven, you are there; if I make my bed in Sheol, you are there.

On the BBC radio programme *Quote Unquote*, I heard a panellist say that on his mother's grave he planned to put her favourite saying: 'That'll do'! For many of us—perhaps, deep down, all of us—this brief life *won't* do. Especially if life is full of sorrows or we are very aware of others' suffering, we are bound to ask, is it 'life's a bitch and then you die'? Do I, or those I love, just disappear?

The Hebrew scriptures say very little about an afterlife. The Old Testament talks about 'Sheol', often translated as 'the grave' and thought of as a shadowy, mysterious underworld. All the dead went down to it, but no one ever came back to report on what it was like.

Yet, now and then, there are extraordinary glimpses of hope for a future world where wrongs would be put right, eternal questions would be answered and humans would see God face to face. Job's cry of faith, in the midst of lamenting his ruined life, is one

such glimpse. Notice how he speaks of seeing God 'in my flesh': in Jewish thought, body and soul cannot live independently (that's a Greek idea)—we are a unity of body, mind and spirit. The image of heaven as a realm of disembodied spirits floating about (or hell as disembodied spirits somehow being tormented) is not a biblical one. Job expects to be recognizably himself, Job, in God's presence.

The psalmist looks at the same idea from another angle. You might expect to find God in heaven—but in hell? Perhaps we need to rethink our talk of hell as being separation from God. There is nowhere in the universe where God is not present.

Sunday reflection

'My Redeemer lives, and at the last he will stand upon the earth.' Let this thought inspire you in your worship today.

VZ

Harvest time

As the people were filled with expectation, and all were questioning in their hearts concerning John, whether he might be the Messiah, John answered all of them by saying, 'I baptize you with water; but one who is more powerful than I is coming; I am not worthy to untie the thong of his sandals. He will baptize you with the Holy Spirit and fire. His winnowing fork is in his hand, to clear his threshing floor and to gather the wheat into his granary; but the chaff he will burn with unquenchable fire.'

In Terry Pratchett's popular *Discworld* fantasy novels, Death, the Grim Reaper, speaks in capital letters. John the Baptist reminds me rather of this character. He's a 'capital letters' sort of man.

John's role is to prepare people for the kingdom of God that Jesus will usher in. His way of doing so is to make them aware of their moral and spiritual (and social) failings. This may sound like 'first, the bad news'. In fact, the announcement that there will be a 'harvest' in which good will be rewarded and evil destroyed is good news. It tells us that all the injustices and sufferings of this wounded earth are going to be put right, that God has a day of reckoning for the oppressor and the exploiter.

As well as this, John makes it clear that we aren't doomed from birth to be either nutritious wheat or tasteless bran. He offers a way that we can begin to change from

bran to wheat: baptism—a physical 'bath' signifying a spiritual desire to be cleansed and start a new life. Even this, however, was nothing to the baptism that Jesus would bring—a baptism that reaches the spiritual parts John's couldn't reach!

Finally, John offers a hint of how the New Testament sees heaven and hell. Those who are fit to live with God are gathered into God's 'grain store' to be used to feed the world. The unfit are destroyed completely, because there is no goodness in them. This gathering and destroying starts now—as we will see tomorrow.

Reflection

Feeling useless? If you have entered God's kingdom by faith and baptism, you are becoming fruitful grain, and God has a use for you.

VZ

Two roads

Enter through the narrow gate; for the gate is wide and the road is easy that leads to destruction, and there are many who take it. For the gate is narrow and the road is hard that leads to life, and there are few who find it.

'Two roads diverged in a wood; / and I, I took the one less travelled by / And that has made all the difference.' Robert Frost's much-loved poem provides the title for M. Scott Peck's bestseller, *The Road Less Travelled*. Peck's book opens with the words, 'Life is difficult'. It is a very Jesus-like sentiment.

We have read how John promised a sorting out of those who were fruitful from those who were mere tasteless, unnourishing 'bran'. Where, though, does this 'great divorce' (in C.S. Lewis' words) start?

In this extract from the collection of teaching known as the Sermon on the Mount, Jesus gives us the image of two roads. The narrow path, with a small gate at its entrance, leads to life, but, because it is hard, few people choose it. You can't get through a narrow gate with a lot of baggage (a bit like that camel trying to get through the eye of a needle)! The other fork of the road has a nice wide entrance, easy to get through, and the road looks like pleasant, straightforward walking.

No wonder the majority take it, but it leads to destruction.

Of course most of those who choose the broad road, do so by default. We may not even know we have chosen it. It is the route of inertia and indifference. The road to hell may not be paved with good intentions so much as with no particular intentions at all.

The two roads hint at an eternal outcome: either life in all its fullness or destruction—being 'unmade'. However, this image is not only about 'life after death'. It is about how we choose to live right now and the impact that has on all around us.

The roads to heaven and hell begin right here on earth, as do the effects of our choice between them. Real life is difficult, but, ultimately, it's the only life there is.

Prayer

Though our road may be narrow, may our minds never be so.

VZ

By their fruits

When the Son of Man comes in his glory, and all the angels with him, then he will sit on the throne of his glory. All the nations will be gathered before him, and he will separate people one from another as a shepherd separates the sheep from the goats, and he will put the sheep at his right hand and the goats at the left. Then the king will say to those at his right hand, 'Come, you that are blessed by my Father, inherit the kingdom prepared for you from the foundation of the world; for I was hungry and you gave me food, I was thirsty and you gave me something to drink, I was a stranger and you welcomed me, I was naked and you gave me clothing, I was sick and you took care of me, I was in prison and you visited me.'

Can you tell sheep from goats? Probably fairly easily, as Western sheep and goats look quite different. Middle Eastern sheep, however, are long-haired and look very similar to goats. You have to bring them together to tell the difference.

So, in this challenging parable, Jesus brings all the people of the earth together to 'compare and contrast' them. This is part of a series of teachings on being ready for the coming kingdom: the story of the slaves awaiting their master's return (24:45–51), the thief who comes in the night (24:43), the wise and foolish bridesmaids (25: 1–13), the servants given money to invest (25:14–30).

Mennonite writer Randy Klassen notes that 'no judgment passage asks anything about the doctrines or beliefs of the individual' (*What Does the Bible Really Say About Hell?*, Pandora Press, 2001). In all these stories, the master, bridegroom or Son of Man is looking for those who have faithfully lived up to their calling (even the thief wants tangible goods!).

Catholic tradition calls the actions described here 'the seven works of mercy'. God does not want duty done with gritted teeth, but for us to show the same kindness and compassion that God has shown us.

We are not saved by our belief, but by grace. Faith is the way in which we come to live under grace. That grace is the foundation of everything good that we do.

Reflection

Have you met Jesus in the needy recently?

VZ

Scary stories

I tell you, many will come from east and west and will eat with Abraham and Isaac and Jacob in the kingdom of heaven, while the heirs of the kingdom will be thrown into the outer darkness, where there will be weeping and gnashing of teeth.

And if your eye causes you to stumble, tear it out; it is better for you to enter the kingdom of God with one eye than to have two eyes and to be thrown into hell, where their worm never dies, and the fire is never quenched.

Do you know the story of the preacher speaking on eternal torment, dwelling especially on the gnashing of teeth? 'I haven't got any teeth,' piped up an old man. 'Teeth,' intoned the preacher, 'will be provided.'

Jesus speaks often of judgment, usually with frightening imagery. Many preachers and teachers have taken this literally, and put 'the fear of God' into their audiences. Medieval churches had wall paintings showing the torments of hell—the horror films of their day. Were they right?

We need to look at some New Testament background. When Jesus speaks of hell, he usually uses the word *Gehenna* (as in today's reading from Mark). The word came from the valley of Hinnom, south of Jerusalem. Here in pagan times, children were burned in sacrifice to Moloch. Later it was a refuse tip and the bodies of the worst criminals were dumped there. So the fire

was continually burning, and the worms, which were hard to exterminate, kept coming back.

This imagery, then, does not *have* to mean that people cast into Gehenna are tormented for ever. It could mean being finally destroyed —the annihilation theory that many biblical scholars believe.

Notice, too, that it's 'the heirs of the kingdom' in Matthew (v. 12) who are thrown into the darkness, while 'many from east and west' are welcomed. God's choice of who goes to life and who to destruction may not be the same as ours. Our calling is to 'work out [our] own salvation with fear and trembling' (Philippians 2:12), sacrificing everything that hinders our progress.

Reflection

Should we speak less of God's anger at sin and more of the love that God has shown us in Christ?

VZ

An empty hell?

For Christ also suffered for sins once for all, the righteous for the unrighteous, in order to bring you to God. He was put to death in the flesh, but made alive in the spirit, in which also he went and made a proclamation to the spirits in prison, who in former times did not obey... For this is the reason the gospel was proclaimed even to the dead, so that, though they had been judged in the flesh as everyone is judged, they might live in the spirit as God does.

Imagine you have fallen into a deep pit and injured yourself so badly that you cannot climb out. Two rescuers arrive. One says, 'Here, I've got a rope ladder; I'll drop it in and you climb up.' The other says, 'I'm coming down with a ladder and I'll carry you up.' Which would you choose?

These strange verses from Peter concern an idea that early theologians developed as 'the harrowing of hell.' You may have seen Orthodox icons where Christ reaches out his hand to help up the 'imprisoned spirits'.

The thought behind this is that there can be nowhere in the universe, physical or spiritual, where Christ's crucified love has not reached. Peter defines the 'spirits who did not obey' as those who were drowned when they refused to enter Noah's ark (v. 20). It is a fitting image for those who, perhaps through ignorance, have failed to follow the call of Christ when they heard it. It might even encompass those who have never heard.

I like this teaching (and so do some scholars). I've long felt that if there is no chance of redemption after death, then God's purpose is defeated by death—which is exactly what the resurrection says it isn't.

So an alternative way of thinking is that hell may, eventually, be empty of all except those who choose to remain there. Even for them, eternity may offer a rescue plan. Hell, in this case, would at the last be destroyed. For those who've been through a few hells on earth, that's quite a promise.

Reflection

'For he must reign until he has put all his enemies under his feet. The last enemy to be destroyed is death' (1 Corinthians 15:25–26). *Let this verse stay in your mind today.*

VZ

Undefeatable

He [Jesus] said to them, 'But who do you say that I am?' Simon Peter answered, 'You are the Messiah, the Son of the living God.' And Jesus answered him, 'Blessed are you, Simon son of Jonah! For flesh and blood has not revealed this to you, but my Father in heaven. And I tell you, you are Peter, and on this rock I will build my church, and the gates of Hades will not prevail against it.'

As I drive my son to school, every day I've been passing a site where an old house has been demolished. A new, very nice (and probably very expensive) house is slowly being built. For months, though, nothing seemed to be happening except preparing the ground and putting in foundations.

For a carpenter, Jesus knew a fair bit about house construction. He knew, for instance, that a good foundation is the key: rock is great, but sand is a bad idea. So he founded his Church—which is the advance guard of God's kingdom—on a rock. That rock was not just Peter the individual (who could be a decidedly 'rocky' character in another sense), but Peter's insight into who Jesus is and what he means.

Many Christians worry about whether or not God really accepts them or they have committed 'the unforgivable sin' (Matthew 12:32). Could I be one of those 'whitewashed tombs' who looks godly, but inside is full of rubbish (Matthew 23:27)? (Yes, actually, but God's doing a clearout job.) Might I be destined for hell or could I be inadvertently possessed by a demon?

Jesus' words to Peter assure us that his body, the Church, is stronger than it may look. If we are 'in Christ',' nothing, not even hell itself, can stand up to us. We are safe.

The image used here is of a walled and gated city under siege by an invading army. To batter down a fortified gate, you need a whole group of people to hold the battering ram. We need to be in this spiritual battle together. That doesn't mean that we all need to think the same, believe the same things and do the same—just that we love and support each other.

Reflection

'Do not fear those who kill the body but cannot kill the soul; rather fear him who can destroy both soul and body in hell.'
(Matthew 10:28)

VZ

MATTHEW 4:17; 13:31–33 (NRSV)

Hidden heaven

From that time Jesus began to proclaim, 'Repent, for the kingdom of heaven has come near.'... He put before them another parable: 'The kingdom of heaven is like a mustard seed that someone took and sowed in his field; it is the smallest of all the seeds, but when it has grown it is the greatest of shrubs and becomes a tree, so that the birds of the air come and make nests in its branches.' He told them another parable: 'The kingdom of heaven is like yeast that a woman took and mixed in with three measures of flour until all of it was leavened.'

Before our son was born, Ed and I used to bake all our own bread (life was easier then...). Now I only do so for special occasions. Recently I got out my 'long life' yeast and made up a batch of dough. After an hour in a cool oven, it still hadn't risen. My yeast had been in the cupboard so long that its life had expired.

'The kingdom of heaven' is a phrase that only occurs in Matthew, the most Jewish of the Gospels. Jews were not allowed to say the name of God (Yahweh), so Matthew found an alternative. The parallel phrase in other Gospels is 'the kingdom of God'.

Jesus portrays this kingdom as something that starts small, like a little piece of yeast or a tiny seed. It is hidden among the dough or in the earth—no one notices it. Yet it will grow into food for many or a home for all the birds.

This teaching is not about some far-off region beyond death. In Jesus, heaven has come near; we can step right into its hinterland. Jews of that time believed in seven heavens, each enclosed in the next. The first was the air around us. So when we pray 'Our Father in heaven', we could think 'Our Father who is as close as the air we breathe'.

When we follow Jesus, we find yeast that never reaches the end of its life.

Sunday reflection

'Not in the dark of buildings confining, Not in some heaven light years away, But here in this place, the new light is shining; Now is the kingdom, now is the day.'

Marty Haugen
© 1982 GIA Publications Inc

VZ

More to life

And he [Jesus] said to them, 'Truly I tell you, there is no one who has left house or wife or brothers or parents or children, for the sake of the kingdom of God, who will not get back very much more in this age, and in the age to come eternal life.'

'Very truly, I tell you, anyone who hears my word and believes him who sent me has eternal life, and does not come under judgment, but has passed from death to life.'

In Douglas Adams' hit radio series and book *The Hitchhiker's Guide to the Galaxy*, robot servants have personality to make them more 'human'. One such is 'Marvin the paranoid android', a permanently depressed character who mutters, 'Life? Don't talk to me about life!'

Jesus, however, does talk about life—much more than he talks about heaven. To a Samaritan woman at a well he promises 'a spring of water gushing up to eternal life' (John 4:14). To the disciples he promises that whatever sacrifices—material, social, emotional—they have made to follow him will be rewarded even in this life. To those who believe what he says about God (which shows in what they do), he says that they are already on the other side of death, living a whole new quality of life.

Paul links this to baptism, saying that we are 'buried with him in baptism' and 'raised with him through faith' (Colossians 2:12). I still remember that feeling of 'Now I have started a new life' as I came up out of the water.

Eternal life starts in the ordinary, not very exciting, sometimes very wearing lives that we lead today. Jesus speaks of salvation in the same way. As Zacchaeus promises to pay back his victims and give half his criminal earnings to the poor, Jesus exclaims, 'Today salvation has come to this house…' (Luke 19:9).

Monday mornings may be a half-alive (or half-dead!) time of the week. Nevertheless, Paul says, although in our struggles we are 'always carrying in the body the death of Jesus', it is 'so that the life of Jesus may also be made visible in our bodies' (2 Corinthians 4:10).

Reflection

'Do not work for the food that perishes, but for the food that endures for eternal life…' (John 6:27). Think on this each day, but particularly Mondays!

VZ

1 CORINTHIANS 15:19–24, 26 (NRSV)

End of the beginning

If for this life only we have hoped in Christ, we are of all people most to be pitied. But in fact Christ has been raised from the dead, the first fruits of those who have died. For since death came through a human being, the resurrection of the dead has also come through a human being; for as all die in Adam, so all will be made alive in Christ. But each in his own order: Christ the first fruits, then at his coming those who belong to Christ. Then comes the end, when he hands over the kingdom to God the Father, after he has destroyed every ruler and every authority and power... The last enemy to be destroyed is death.

When I hear people say 'Charity begins at home', I always want to ask, 'But need it end there?'

Eternal life begins now, but if it ends there, our hope isn't very great. Christians, just like others, go through poverty, illness and the breakdown of relationships, but 'hope does not disappoint us, because God's love has been poured into our hearts through the Holy Spirit...' (Romans 5:5). That Holy Spirit in us is a 'first instalment' of our heavenly heritage (2 Corinthians 1:22), a 'seal for the day of redemption' (Ephesians 4:30). Our hope is for the present and the future (and even the past, as God by the Spirit heals past hurts).

More than that, our hope is not merely an individual one in which God saves people 'like a brand plucked from the fire' (Zechariah 3:2—a favourite verse of John Wesley, who was rescued from a house fire as a child). Even this verse refers to all of God's people and, in today's reading, we have an extraordinary promise: that 'all will be made alive in Christ' (1 Corinthians 15:22). Some take this to mean that all people will eventually recognize Christ and live. It is certainly a picture of a far-reaching redemption, in which all powers that defy God will eventually be destroyed.

Reflection

After a great Allied victory in World War II, Churchill said, 'This is not the end. It is not even the beginning of the end; but it is, perhaps, the end of the beginning.' We could say something similar of our hope in Christ.

VZ

Only Jesus

One of the criminals who were hanged there kept deriding him and saying, 'Are you not the Messiah? Save yourself and us!' But the other rebuked him, saying, 'Do you not fear God, since you are under the same sentence of condemnation? And we indeed have been condemned justly, for we are getting what we deserve for our deeds, but this man has done nothing wrong.' Then he said, 'Jesus, remember me when you come into your kingdom.' He replied, 'Truly I tell you, today you will be with me in Paradise.'

Ed and I just came back yesterday from a weekend trip to Brussels. One thing I put carefully in a safe place was our airport car park ticket. That was our means of getting home.

I'm not keen on 'ticket to heaven' images of faith. They can imply that as long as we've signed on the dotted line of some confession of faith, nothing else need happen. God looks for godly actions as evidence of our faith— just as our local education authority is asking that I bring to the special needs tribunal some evidence of my belief that our son needs a statement of special needs.

The condemned burglar in our reading, however, has no history of love to take with him to the cross —nothing except his recognition that, in Jesus, a new kingdom has arrived, a kingdom not defeated even by death. Yet Jesus, without hesitation, promises him paradise and more—to be 'with me' (v. 43).

We may be judged by our actions, but we are not saved by them. God will examine how we have built on the foundation of Jesus—'with gold, silver, precious stones, wood, hay, straw' (1 Corinthians 3:12)—and 'If what has been built on the foundation survives, the builder will receive a reward' (3:14). Nevertheless, even though our good works are few and feeble, if we belong to Jesus we will still be saved (3:15). Ultimately, we need nothing but a love of Jesus and a desire to follow him wherever he goes. Where he's going is to a new world, of which we can be a part.

Reflection

It is correct to say 'God is love'; it is wrong to say 'God is wrath' (Randy Klassen). Praise God for the mercy that you have received.

VZ

Being agnostic

But someone will ask, 'How are the dead raised? With what kind of body do they come?' Fool! What you sow does not come to life unless it dies. And as for what you sow, you do not sow the body that is to be, but a bare seed, perhaps of wheat or of some other grain. But God gives it a body as he has chosen, and to each kind of seed its own body... Listen, I will tell you a mystery! We will not all die, but we will all be changed, in a moment, in the twinkling of an eye, at the last trumpet. For the trumpet will sound, and the dead will be raised imperishable, and we will be changed. For this perishable body must put on imperishability, and this mortal body must put on immortality.

My son's teacher has brought a butterfly hatchery into the classroom. Each little perspex pot contains a caterpillar and all the food it will need until it spins its cocoon. If you could ask the caterpillar what will happen when it comes out of that cocoon, I'm sure it would have no idea. No butterfly has ever come back to tell it about flying!

Today is Ascension Day, when we remember the risen Jesus returning to God and no longer being visible to his disciples. Where is Jesus now? What does it mean that he, who was human, is part of God's very being, the Trinity?

When Ed and I travel by car, the driver generally lets the passenger navigate. To go on a journey into the unknown, you only need to trust your guide. Jesus trusted his Father and we can trust Jesus. We don't need to know more.

One thing we can know about the new heaven and new earth is that, in some way, it will resemble the universe we now inhabit. Paul talks in terms of a risen body—something that can sense, feed and love.

Last night I saw on television a woman who, as a result of a rare virus, had lost all sense of touch. Unable to feel the ground, she couldn't walk, and every daily task was a feat of hand-eye co-ordination. She was effectively 'disembodied'. Heaven will not be like that.

Prayer
*Jesus, give me all the spiritual food
I need to grow my wings.*

VZ

MATTHEW 13:24–30 (NRSV, ABRIDGED)

Not our job

He [Jesus] put before them another parable: 'The kingdom of heaven may be compared to someone who sowed good seed in his field; but while everybody was asleep, an enemy came and sowed weeds among the wheat, and then went away. So when the plants came up and bore grain, then the weeds appeared as well... The slaves said to him, "Then do you want us to go and gather them?" But he replied, "No; for in gathering the weeds you would uproot the wheat along with them. Let both of them grow together until the harvest; and at harvest time I will tell the reapers, Collect the weeds first and bind them in bundles to be burned, but gather the wheat into my barn." '

A friend at church is offering everyone a self-set ash tree from his garden. No one has taken up the offer; they have enough uninvited ash and sycamore saplings in their own gardens!

We may disagree about whether or not weeds are an invention of Satan. (I've always rather liked bindweed flowers—but not on my roses!) The real problem with the weeds in today's reading is that, until everything is fully grown, you cannot tell green field grass from green wheat.

Remember that the whole field here belongs to the farmer, just as the whole world belongs to God. There will be inedible, uninvited grass in God's wheat field, but we are not the ones appointed to tell the difference. We might be so zealous in pulling up weeds that we destroy some perfectly good wheat (does that sound at all like

any incidents in Church history?)

Roger Wagner's stunning painting 'The harvest is the end of the age, and the reapers are angels' shows a ripe cornfield with powerful winged figures setting their sickles to the stalks of the grain. There is a harvest; but we are not the reapers.

Reflection

'But woe to you, scribes and Pharisees, hypocrites! For you lock people out of the kingdom of heaven. For you do not go in yourselves, and when others are going in, you stop them... you cross sea and land to make a single convert, and you make the new convert twice as much a child of hell as yourselves' (Matthew 23:13 –15). *Let us not lock the door too hastily.*

VZ

REVELATION 20:14—21:5 (NRSV, ABRIDGED)

Free at last

Then Death and Hades were thrown into the lake of fire. This is the second death, the lake of fire; and anyone whose name was not found written in the book of life was thrown into the lake of fire. Then I saw a new heaven and a new earth; for the first heaven and the first earth had passed away... And I saw the holy city, the new Jerusalem, coming down out of heaven from God, prepared as a bride adorned for her husband... And the one who was seated on the throne said, 'See, I am making all things new.'

Why a new heaven as well as a new earth? What was wrong with the old one? 'Heaven' in the Bible can mean simply 'sky', so this could mean a whole new universe. However, 'heaven' can also mean 'God's realm'. This passage may be saying that heaven has not been created yet, that it will be ushered in at the end of time. Christians do not believe in the immortality of the soul—the spirit living on separately from the dead body—but in resurrection of the body 'on the last day'.

Of course, as American author and speaker Tony Campolo points out, God is outside time, so, when that day comes, the distinction between now and the future will be meaningless. The kingdom of God (which Jesus talked about far more than heaven) is both now *and* to come. Then, death will be among the things that have 'passed away'. Now, death is still among us, but it is defeated.

The important thing for us now is to live, by God's Spirit, as if the kingdom is already here. Jesus gave Peter 'the keys of the kingdom of heaven' and said 'whatever you bind on earth will be bound in heaven, and whatever you loose on earth will be loosed in heaven' (Matthew 16:19). We are God's heavenly delegates, and our actions of imprisoning or freeing have eternal consequences. We should major on freeing people, imprisoning only the forces of evil.

Reflection

'Do not be afraid; I am the first and the last, and the living one. I was dead, and see, I am alive forever and ever; and I have the keys of Death and of Hades.'
(Revelation 1:17–18)

VZ

29

Romans 8

'Exciting', 'important' and 'necessary' are three words that come to my mind as I think about Romans chapter 8. 'Neglected' would be another! Why do I say that?

During my years as a Christian, different passages of scripture have dominated our understanding of the Holy Spirit and his ministry. First, it was the teaching given by Jesus about the Spirit in John's Gospel—in particular, exploring the connection between the Spirit and Jesus and the way that the Spirit could help us to bridge two thousand years of history. Also around was a fascination with the 'fruit of the Spirit' mentioned in Galatians 5:22, seeking to highlight the distinctive Christ-like characteristics. Then came 1 Corinthians 12—14, with its relevance to 'body ministry' and charismatic gifts, which had for so long been sidelined in mainstream churches. Flowing out of this was an emphasis on healing, words of knowledge and prayers of faith, for which the books of Luke and Acts became important demonstrative texts.

All these parts of the scriptures and the insights that they give, enabling us to live more Spirit-filled lives, are valuable and valid, but, in the past 40 or so years, a key passage seems to me to have been relatively dormant. Yet it is powerful and comprehensive—Romans 8.

Romans 8 is a very rich exploration of the ministry of the Holy Spirit. It is not only valuable for individuals, or even just within the Church of Jesus Christ, but also extends to cover the relevance of the Holy Spirit throughout all creation. At a time when ecological concerns are recognized by many more Christians as 'kingdom territory', perhaps Romans 8 will enable us to engage more readily with its message.

The importance of this passage is not, of course, determined by its felt relevance to our needs! It can be seen quite clearly from the structure of Paul's great letter. The Holy Spirit has received almost no overt recognition until this point and now occurs in almost every verse. As we read, we will rediscover just how exciting, important and necessary the Holy Spirit really is.

In order to gain the full benefit from this fortnight's readings, I suggest that each day you read the verses from the day before and the day after as well as the one for that day.

David Spriggs

The Spirit brings life

If you belong to Christ Jesus, you won't be punished. The Holy Spirit will give you life that comes from Christ Jesus and will set you free from sin and death.

The Holy Spirit is the one through whom we experience the grace of God, by whom we are empowered to live out the life of God and with whom we are enabled to live for God. If this sounds rather theoretical and vague, please don't be anxious for we shall soon discover that Romans chapter 8 is full of spiritual and practical riches. As we begin our readings with this chapter, however, it is important to paint at least part of the big picture that Paul gives us. So here goes!

The Holy Spirit is the one who turns the theory of Christian theology into daily Christian experience. For the Christian, there need be no gap between the questions 'Is it true?' and 'Does it work?' The Holy Spirit is the one whom God has given the role of ensuring that his truth works for us. We are meant to experience the difference the Holy Spirit makes in all kinds of ways and in all manner of situations. That is why Paul writes, 'The Holy Spirit will give you life' (v. 2) —not death in terms of a diminution of human freedoms, nor even life in terms of some religious code of behaviour or private morality, but full, expansive human, relational and civil life.

The Holy Spirit is not some kind of general life force, however. To avoid this dangerous and tempting assumption, Paul makes two strong links between the Holy Spirit and Jesus Christ. First, the empowering of the Holy Spirit is not available generally. It is only possible in its fullness for those who 'belong to Christ Jesus' (v. 1). Second, the difference in the quality of life we can experience is not general enhancement or ecstasy, nor even moral strength. Rather, it is the life that comes from, and so mirrors, that of Christ Jesus.

So, if we want to experience more of the reality of Jesus and express more of him to others, this chapter gives us the opportunity we are looking for.

Sunday reflection

'Holy Spirit, fill my life with Jesus; fill my heart with his love' (Romans 5:5). Start to imagine what this will feel like for you and others.

DS

Roadside assistance?

The Law of Moses cannot do this, because our selfish desires make the Law weak. But God set you free when he sent his own Son to be like us sinners and to be a sacrifice for our sin. God used Christ's body to condemn sin. He did this, so that we would do what the Law commands by obeying the Spirit instead of our own desires. People who are ruled by their desires think only of themselves. Everyone who is ruled by the Holy Spirit thinks about spiritual things.

Picture a familiar sight. As you journey by road, you see a car that has broken down. Perhaps it is one ready for the scrapheap, perhaps it is a new, expensive one. Beside it is a breakdown services van.

No matter how brilliant the design and no matter how expensive the car, a flaw or a failure means it cannot move. According to Paul, the Law of Moses was a brilliant gift—indeed, a divine gift. It was the top of the range, the best that God could provide to direct and help us live in a way that would most bless human society and most please God. However, because of flaws in us, there is a breakdown. No matter how many times we try to start it, no matter how hard we press the accelerator, it will not move, so our lives remain a sorry story of failure and frustration.

So what does God do? To continue with our analogy, he sends the breakdown service. Jesus comes and, through his life and sacrificial death, there is the possibility of a new start. The Holy Spirit is the one who sorts things out: he diagnoses the problem and supplies the answer; he mends us so that we can work as we were meant to.

Unlike our earthly breakdown service, however, there is no signing off. The Holy Spirit becomes part of our lives, our constant companion to ensure that the fatal flaw never gets the upper hand again. The Holy Spirit becomes a new centre of consciousness for us, whose focus is naturally on God and not, as in our own unaided case, our own needs.

Prayer

Father, help me to see where your Holy Spirit makes a difference to my thinking and acting today.

DS

Tuesday 25 May

ROMANS 8:6–8 (CEV)

The battle for the mind

If our minds are ruled by our desires, we will die. But if our minds are ruled by the Spirit, we will have life and peace. Our desires fight against God, because they do not and cannot obey God's laws. If we follow our desires, we cannot please God.

Recently I heard of a Christian conference that was held at a hotel. Afterwards, the hotel noticed that more of the guests had used Channel 5 (the pornography channel) than would be the case while the rooms were occupied by secular businessmen. Basic lust was clearly still operating powerfully in this Christian group.

Lust is by no means the only way in which our desires are expressed, nor the only way in which they fight against God! Paul's list of the desires of the flesh in Galatians makes very challenging reading for us all.

Gossip, greed and gluttony could also be added to such a list and, in different ways, each can be devastating for the people involved.

The question prompted by my opening story is whether or not such Christian people are ruled by their desires. Initially it looks that way, but I suspect that many of them would have had an inner struggle over whether or not to watch such programmes before switching channels, and they would have felt considerable guilt afterwards, just as they would feel if they

lapsed into gossip or greed. That kind of struggle indicates that we are going against something and that something is the Holy Spirit, to whom we have surrendered our own natural desires and preferences.

The greater danger is when we habitually participate in thoughts or actions that are contrary to the love, purity and goodwill that characterize the rule of the Holy Spirit. Then we wear down the beneficial impact of the Spirit, our internal God-given resistance.

That is why many of the great Christians down the ages encourage us to keep short accounts with God—to honestly and openly review our weaknesses and sins and acknowledge them for what they really are. That is why the saints challenge us to holiness—the natural outcome of the supernatural presence of God's Spirit.

Reflection

Read Galatians 5:19–21, ask God to show you where you are vulnerable and invite the Holy Spirit to start to transform you.

DS

ROMANS 8:9 (CEV)

What's in these names?

You are no longer ruled by your desires, but by God's Spirit, who lives in you. People who don't have the Spirit of Christ in them don't belong to him.

Already, in these first few verses, we have had four different ways of referring to the Holy Spirit. We should pause and reflect on them all, for together they provide us with a rich understanding of him. Different people call me by different names—and these are only the ones that they use to my face! 'Mr Spriggs' usually indicates they do not know me very well—it is rather formal, but shows the family to which I belong. My friends call me 'David' and that is comfortable and welcoming. 'The Reverend Dr David Spriggs' implies both that I am a Christian minister and that I did some studying. So, what might be the tone of voice used for the names Paul mentions?

When he uses 'Spirit', which is fairly rare, he is indicating the kind of reality that he is dealing with—not a person with a physical presence, nor a deity in some distant realm, but a mysterious, powerful, superhuman presence. Of course, there were many kinds of 'spirit' that people thought about, so often he is more specific. On the other hand, the way in which he uses 'Spirit' does imply that, for the Christian, there is only one 'Spirit' who really matters.

The normal way to refer to this being is as the 'Holy Spirit'. This tells us something about the origin and function of this spirit. He is not dark and dangerous, but comes from a divine realm, and contact with him links us to God. 'The Spirit of God' underlines this connection with God, but often has the additional nuance of reminding us that the Spirit is a gift from God.

Perhaps the most vivid and intimate name Paul uses is the 'Spirit of Christ'. In a wonderful way, this fills out and brings into focus the rather vague picture that even 'Holy Spirit' conveys. The link to Jesus indicates qualities of warmth, compassion, cleansing, healing, hope and deep understanding of and caring about our predicaments because that's how Jesus was on earth and that's how he is in heaven.

Reflection

Which name do you prefer for the Holy Spirit and what does that indicate about your relationship with the Spirit?

DS

Christ's kind of life

But Christ lives in you. So you are alive because God has accepted you, even though your bodies must die because of your sins. Yet God raised Jesus to life! God's Spirit now lives in you, and he will raise you to life by his Spirit. My dear friends, we must not live to satisfy our desires. If you do, you will die. But you will live, if by the help of God's Spirit you say 'No' to your desires.

As though to emphasize the inseparability of Jesus and the Spirit, Paul can say both that 'Christ lives in you' and 'God's Spirit now lives in you' (vv. 10, 11). This indicates clearly the Christ-shaped qualities of character, attitudes and behaviour that are appropriate for Christian people and should be our hallmark (see Galatians 5:22–25 or, indeed, 1 Corinthians 13:4–7 where many people have spotted a pen portrait of Jesus, even though his name is not mentioned). For all those who feel that they are victims of their own upbringing or emotions, this is gospel—good news—the promise that we can be set free and empowered to live a beautiful and creative life. To reach this Christ-like life is, nevertheless, going to be a struggle and sometimes as Christians we fail and need support and help.

Now, though, Paul brings in another, completely different dimension—that of resurrection life. Just as personal corruption is a reality we all struggle with, in spite of our Christian commitment, so is physical death. However, this does not undermine Paul's claims either. Jesus died, but God raised him to life and his life is the pattern for all believers. Yes, we will die; but yes, we will live on the other side of physical death. The reasonable basis for this claim is that God's Spirit, who is indestructible, lives in us and so God will raise us to life by his Spirit in us, just as he did with Jesus. This, too, is good news.

Reflection

In the development of a Christ-like life, we have an absolutely necessary part to play—saying 'No' to our human instincts. Life on the other side of death, however, is entirely God's doing.

DS

The best news of all

Only those people who are led by God's Spirit are his children. God's Spirit doesn't make us slaves who are afraid of him. Instead, we become his children and call him our Father.

The people of Israel had been made slaves in Egypt. Slavery is a state of degradation and misery—the loss of every aspect of freedom, reward, dignity and aspiration. It is worse than a living death—indeed, it is the denial of all God made us for. God sent Moses to lead his people out of slavery, but following Moses was a hazardous business and it took courage to leave the misery that they knew for an uncertain future. How did people know he was not leading them into an even more devastating form of slavery? Yet, the only way they could gain their freedom was to follow Moses. If they stayed behind in Egypt they were doomed. If they chose to deviate from Moses' route, they were lost.

Paul sees us as slaves to our base desires, and the only way to freedom is to follow God's Spirit. Those who do are God's children, because God's Spirit lives in them as well as leads them. To be led by the Spirit is not about going somewhere different; it is about being someone different. Using a more modern image, we could say that the Spirit's 'DNA' reshapes our lives from the inside out. Having the Spirit's 'DNA' marks us out 'genetically' as belonging to God, being his children.

However, the Spirit does not enslave us like some alien force taking over our minds and directing us to do anything the alien chooses. The Spirit is not a terrifying monster inhabiting the control centre of our lives—just the opposite! God pours his love into our hearts through the Spirit (Romans 5:5) and that love is, of course, the love of a Father for his children. So, we are given the right to call God Father.

Reflection

'Yet some people accepted him and put their faith in him. So he gave them the right to be the children of God. They were not God's children by nature or because of any human desires. God himself was the one who made them his children.'
(John 1:12–13)

DS

Becoming sure

God's Spirit makes us sure that we are his children. His Spirit lets us know that together with Christ we will be given what God has promised. We will also share in the glory of Christ, because we have suffered with him.

There is a vast difference between being God's children and being sure that we are God's children. God gives us his Spirit so that we can experience the joyful reality of being his children as well as the benefits, which are ours as a result of this. The Spirit helps to make us certain.

If you have ever been in any kind of serious danger, then you will understand what I mean. Imagine that you have been at sea in a small sailboat and unexpectedly a massive storm blows up. The sails are in tatters, the land is completely obliterated by the heavy rain and the waves that constantly break over the boat and soak you. This goes on for hour after hour, and all you can do is lash yourself to the boat. Then a lifeboat appears and you are in the reassuring company of the crew, who wrap you up in a dry blanket and, within minutes, you are safe on dry land. Wonderful! Until you close your eyes, that is, and then the danger through which you have just passed returns to overwhelm you. The memories and emotions you have lived with for hours are more dominant than the reality of safety. The nightmares may even last for years.

Being rescued by God from our own sin and having our fears about him released by his love does not mean that in an instant we can truly feel that we are his children. There will be moments when it may be easy to experience what Paul says—that we are his children and can call him Father. Equally, there may well be hours and days when our past experience dominates our present awareness. The Holy Spirit will never give us up, but stays to work within our very being to convince us.

Prayer

Holy Spirit, remind me that crucifixion leads to resurrection, resurrection to ascension and ascension to the restoration of the universe. Remind me, too, that my struggles are the proof that I belong to Christ in both suffering and glory.

DS

Spoilt by suffering?

I am sure that what we are suffering now cannot compare with the glory that will be shown to us.

Does this strike you as a disappointment? We have reached the pinnacle of celebrating the fact that, by God's Spirit, we have become his children—such an enormous privilege. We have even looked beyond this pinnacle to the fulfilment of our lives as we glimpse the reality of spending eternity with God—sharing in the glory of God. So why does Paul have to spoil it by bringing us back to 'suffering'?

Part of the answer is that Paul was a realist! Many of us live in a culture that values the minimization of suffering and we have pills for everything from headaches to mood swings. We anaesthetize ourselves with wall-to-wall sound or television or seductive advertising, but pain and suffering are still an unavoidable experience for everyone, just as they were for the Son of God.

For the Christian, however, there are other dimensions to this suffering. Thinking that Christianity is a prop for strugglers is nonsense. In fact, the reverse is commonly the case. Choosing to be a Christian is a recipe for difficulties because it inevitably brings responsibilities and antagonisms. Jesus warned that people will persecute us if we follow him. We must put others first and refuse to retaliate when attacked or harmed. We are called to do right even when it is not convenient or personally beneficial. We also suffer internal struggles because, as Paul indicated earlier, we have to crush our selfish desires and allow God's way to dominate our agendas.

Furthermore, Christians experience deep suffering because they share with God the tension between a sinful and distorted world and the world as God intends it to be. This dimension of restlessness with what is—because we know what could, and one day will be—is what drives Paul to share the gospel to the ends of the earth. He knows that, until that has happened, God cannot bring his purposes to their glorious conclusion (see Matthew 24:14).

The measure of our suffering, multiplied a thousand times, is the mirror of his glory.

Sunday prayer

As we meet with your people, Lord, may we be strengthened by the knowledge that the glory we will have is far greater than all the suffering we endure.

DS

Hard labour or labour pains?

In fact, all creation is eagerly waiting for God to show who his children are. Meanwhile, creation is confused, but not because it wants to be confused. God made it this way in the hope that creation would be set free from decay and would share in the glorious freedom of his children. We know that all creation is still groaning and is in pain, like a woman about to give birth.

The world is not as peaceful and fulfilling as it could be. We can perceive suffering and tension not only within our human lives, but deeply embedded and evasively permeating the whole of creation. The struggle of plants and animals for survival or the natural but disturbing process of one species feeding off another are vivid reminders. However, this sense of 'dis-ease' extends into the inanimate realms as well, illustrating this problem—the violence of tidal waves that rush inland causing destruction of all in their path or, from earth's early history, asteroids creating huge explosions.

How are we to respond to such phenomena? Paul uses words such as 'confusion', 'decay' and 'groaning in pain', which provide us with a perceptive framework and certainly capture some of my responses. Are such responses justified, however?

If they were only natural processes, surely not—they would simply be harsh reality. Why, then, do we have this profound sense of 'dis-ease' with the way the world is? Seeing such disasters as the outworkings of God's curse on Adam and the earth take us so far—for these tensions and violence certainly do not reflect God's initial plan, but neither are they God's final harsh condemnation. They are a temporary state leading on to something wonderful, just as the labour pains of a woman are not an end in themselves but lead to the joy of holding a new life in her arms. In this case, however, it is not the natural birth of a single child into this world, but the new state of all God's children in his new world. Somehow, our 'revelation' as God's children will bring restoration to the cosmos.

Prayer

Lord God, helps us to glimpse your glorious purposes for us and all creation, and may that glimpse enable us to live through the sufferings around us and bring your light and hope to others.

DS

Not yet, but not long!

The Spirit makes us sure about what we will be in the future. But now we groan silently, while we wait for God to show that we are his children. This means that our bodies will also be set free. And this hope is what saves us. But if we already have what we hope for, there is no need to keep on hoping. However, we hope for something we have not yet seen, and we patiently wait for it.

'Trust in the Lord, wait patiently for him' was the psalmist's appeal. Whether it is for a train that is late or the delivery of the latest technological wizardry, we are not a waiting generation. We expect to have everything now. There are some things, however, that even we cannot hurry—the gestation period for a baby, for instance! Such, according to Paul, is also the case for our 'revelation' as God's children.

Apparently we are not the only generation to have found it hard to wait. The New Testament suggests that some people thought that the resurrection of all believers, as well as Jesus, had already happened. Here it looks as though Paul was responding to those who sensed that they were already fully God's children, perhaps because of the profound impact of the Holy Spirit on their lives. Paul maintains that the best is still to come and this is infinitely greater, better and more glorious than even the privileges of being his children now.

At present, we are still in the womb of the current age. We exist, but we cannot be seen by others. Also, not all our faculties are functioning and we can't perceive the full reality of God and his universe any more than can a baby in the womb. When the time is right, we shall be fully delivered, 'our bodies will also be set free' (v. 23), we shall share Christ's glory and the universe will be released too. Although being a child of God is a deeply intimate, personally transforming work of God's Holy Spirit, the ultimate outcome is of cosmic significance. We can only glimpse what this might mean, but we must not give up on this rich hope.

Reflection

If the universe is several billion years old, then 2000 years is not really very long, is it?

DS

Not alone!

In certain ways we are weak, but the Spirit is here to help us. For example, when we don't know what to pray for, the Spirit prays for us in ways that cannot be put into words. All our thoughts are known to God. He can understand what is in the mind of the Spirit, as the Spirit prays for God's people.

Aliens, UFOs, *The X-Files*... humans seem unable to avoid the sense that there is something else 'out there' wanting to communicate with us, alluring us into some kind of relationship, probably aiming for our own, as well as the planet's, destruction.

In certain ways, the human race is strong—in exploration, communication, artistic expression, technological development, caring for the environment, building community. In other ways we are vulnerable—given to violence, exploiting developments for evil and control, subject to viruses, failing to foresee the destructive potential of even our own developments, ageing, death.

As Christians, we are aware of other weaknesses. While we know that there is a fuller and richer future to come, we can neither bring it about, nor even paint a very clear picture of it. This leaves us vulnerable when we talk to other people about such things, but also when it comes to our own patient waiting. Patient waiting means living in a high state of readiness,

remaining committed and focused on shaping our lives according to it, just as if we are expecting a terrorist attack or someone to deliver a cheque for six million pounds to our house—as long as we are there!

However, the good news is that we are not alone. There is a God who is ceaselessly at work to bring about the glorious future, and his very presence, the Holy Spirit, is here to help us. So, when we fail to show Christ's character, when we mess up with God, when the pain of creation, friends or ourselves dominates our horizons or even when God's wonderful purposes for us and the universe seem to have floated far out of reach, the Holy Spirit is there for us. He brings our hidden longings and buried aspirations to God; he rekindles the wonder of God's present love and the dream of God's future in our hearts. He will never let us fade away.

Prayer

Lord, teach me to wait patiently and live gloriously.

DS

Destination known

We know that God is always at work for the good of everyone who loves him. They are the ones God has chosen for his purpose, and he has always known who his chosen ones would be. He had decided to let them become like his own Son, so that his Son would be the first of many children. God then accepted the people he had already decided to choose and he has shared his glory with them.

God is ceaselessly, and in every set of circumstances, actively and purposefully at work on our behalf. Through the Holy Spirit, he is transforming us into Christ-like people. This promise, however, also applies to the circumstances that appear to shape decisively (and often mis-shape) our lives.

Unemployment, childlessness or too many children, illness or a car accident may seem to us like dominating events that leave us as victims, struggling like a fish dangling on the hook at the end of the fisherman's line. 'No!' claims Paul. God is in there with you. He shares your pain as any caring father would—he doesn't turn his back on you as a redundant employee or a captured soldier whose well-being lies in the hands of the commander-in-chief. Yet, even more than this, God is involved in sorting out the circumstances or in enabling us, together with him, to circumvent and redeem those circumstances, so becoming 'more than conquerors' (v. 37, NRSV).

Certainly, it is not always easy to see how God is at work for our good and, unless we reckon on a world where not only people but also the very structure of the cosmos are out of sorts, it is difficult to make any sense of the complexities of life. Given that creation is in travail, however, and given our past experiences and the testimony of many notable Christians throughout history, it is a reasonable and helpful view. Nor should we forget that this was Paul's view and he had been through most things and knew that he could even go through death and it would still be vibrantly true.

It is, I think, the existence of the Holy Spirit that means God can 'underwrite' this promise. Stay in touch with him!

Reflection

Think of times where, working with God, you have seen painful circumstances redeemed.

DS

God has done it!

What can we say about all this? If God is on our side, can anyone be against us? God did not keep back his own Son, but he gave him for us. If God did this, won't he freely give us everything else? If God says his chosen ones are acceptable to him, can anyone bring charges against them? Or can anyone condemn them? No indeed! Christ died and was raised to life, and now he is at God's right side, speaking to him for us.

Yesterday, we looked at some powerful reasons for believing that God is at work for our good, when so much that is happening to us and around us seems to contradict this. We left aside the most powerful argument of all, however—the fact that God has visibly demonstrated this commitment to our well-being in Jesus.

Before we return to this central plank in both Paul's argument and his experience, it is worth pausing to consider his question—'If God is on our side, who can be against us?' Experience suggests that the answer is 'all kinds'! Job's experience is a mystery to himself and his friends, but for the reader it is clear that Satan, 'The Accuser', is against Job, not God. For a Christian in Rome, the answer to Paul's question might have included Jews and maybe even Caesar, for the claim 'Jesus is Lord' would be thought of as rebellion. To those who were slaves, the answer was probably 'my master'

and to wives, often 'my husband'. Paul knew all this very well, but he also believed that God had issued a divine decree that he was on our side—we are justified. So, Paul is not painting a picture of a trouble-free life, but justification, being right with God.

God has not only demonstrated his commitment to us by offering Jesus as the means of our redemption but has also shown his ability to deliver on his commitment! The resurrection is the demonstration of this divine capacity. Not even death can intervene, for Christ has overcome the finality of death. Even more than that, Jesus has broken through the barrier, creating a cosmic hole for us to pass through, and is using his resurrection life to support us (v. 34).

Prayer

Lord, help me to know
that you are working for me in
today's circumstances.

DS

The still centre

Can anything separate us from the love of Christ? Can trouble, suffering, and hard times, or hunger and nakedness, or danger and death? It is exactly as the Scriptures say, 'For you we face death all day long. We are like sheep on their way to be butchered.' In everything we have won more than a victory because of Christ who loves us. I am sure that nothing can separate us from God's love—not life or death, not angels or spirits, not the present or the future, and not powers above or powers below. Nothing in all creation can separate us from God's love for us in Christ Jesus our Lord!

Paul had often faced death; he was often in a 'powerless' position with respect to political, physical and spiritual powers (see Acts 16: 16–23; 23:23—24:27; 27:13–44). He could write, without needing to justify it, that 'We are fighting against forces and authorities and against rulers of darkness and powers in the spiritual world' (Ephesians 6:12). Additionally, people living in the pagan world were terrified by the unpredictable whim of gods and rulers (both small and large).

We can perhaps understand their feelings if we contemplate growing older. We may fear having less control over our own lives, dread becoming dependent on people's support, eventually requiring help with feeding, washing, dressing and mobility. Government decisions about funding for care homes and nursing are made over our heads, but their impact reaches deep into our lives.

How can we live surrounded by such a terrifying crowd of unpredictable events and malevolent forces? Paul's answer takes us to the heart of the universe. The heart of the universe, however, is not millions of light years away, it is intimately near to us. It cannot be glimpsed through the most powerful astronomical telescope, but it can be experienced by the simplest believer. For the heart of the universe is God's love, demonstrated for us by Jesus.

Reflection

When we doubt because of the oppressive nature of our life experience, we need to journey to the sacramental table and taste again the bread and wine and all they bring to us. There, God holds us gently, but with the divine strength of crucified love.

DS

Power and authority

Everyone has experience of power and authority. At work, in law, in the family, in the Church, we come across people who lead, whose opinion, position and actions affect the lives of others. Most of us have exercised authority ourselves in one sphere or another. All of us have lived under other people's leadership, for at least part of our lives. Power and authority are often used well, but sometimes they are carried very badly. Like fire, these gifts must be handled with care.

So, what does the Bible say? The first of our readings looks at the power of God. On Trinity Sunday, we reflect on God as Father, Son and Holy Spirit, powerfully at work in our lives. Then, through the first week, we read some Old Testament passages. We start with creation and the Ten Commandments, and the authority they have to frame the way in which we live. We go on to look at responsible people in Israel's life—prophet, king and priest. Then our Old Testament section ends with Daniel's vision of the Son of Man, receiving authority from God over all the nations.

Our New Testament readings in the second week begin with that same Son of Man as he comes to us in the person of Jesus. We ask, 'By what authority did Jesus act?' We hear of Herod Antipas and Pontius Pilate. They were the powerful men of Jesus' time, although neither carried his position very creditably and their uneasy actions contrast with the steady authority of person and spirit that Jesus showed.

We look at the leadership of Paul as missionary and apostle and of the Council of Jerusalem in sorting out a church dispute by patiently speaking and listening. Romans 13 explores the purpose of human government and how it can promote peace and goodness. Then, our final passage, like the last of our Old Testament readings, describes a vision. It tells of the risen Christ, who appears as a wounded Lamb in John's great vision of Revelation, to receive honour, power and praise.

The word these Bible readings have impressed on me is 'responsibility'. Power and authority involve trust. When we hold them we are responsible—for the job itself, to the people who gave it to us, to the people we serve and, ultimately, to God. To hold power is to hold a question mark in our hands: how are we responding to this trust? Are we trustworthy?

John Proctor

45

EPHESIANS 3:14–17 (NRSV, ABRIDGED)

Trinity of love and power

I bow my knees before the Father, from whom every family in heaven and on earth takes its name. I pray that, according to the riches of his glory, he may grant that you may be strengthened in your inner being with power through his Spirit, and that Christ may dwell in your hearts through faith, as you are being rooted and grounded in love.

Christians have long believed in God as Trinity, as one God in three persons—Father, Son and Holy Spirit. The New Testament never spells out this idea. Yet many passages in the New Testament seem to reach for this way of understanding and worshipping God. From very early on, Christians knew their God in this way and with this faith. We see it here, in this great prayer from Ephesians.

The prayer is all about power, God's power in the lives of Christian people. Here is God the Father and Creator, from whom we receive all that is good in our human relationships. God has dreamt, designed and shaped our humanity and now his creative strength is lovingly shared with those who trust him.

Here, too, is the power of God the Holy Spirit—gentle breath who stirs and animates our living, flame who kindles our love for God and neighbour. Here is the counsellor, defender and comforter, prompting our desires, sustaining and sup-

porting us under pressure, giving courage for the challenges ahead.

Here also is the presence of God the Son, keeping company with the Christian, guiding and guarding us from within. The Christ of pardon and promise, of cross and resurrection, dwells in our hearts, knowing our thoughts and concerns and sharing his with us. To know Christ within gives depth to our being and firm security in his love. Roots and foundations, ground and growth, stability and energy are ours in Jesus.

The power of God is intimate, personal, generous—and Trinitarian. The three-in-one God shares his life with us. Trinity is not just a theory, a way of looking at God—it is a way of living with God, knowing God and experiencing God's power.

Sunday prayer

Pray today's prayer, as Paul did, for friends of yours, that they too may know more fully the generous power of God.

JP

Living up to your image

Then God said, 'Let us make humankind in our image, according to our likeness; and let them have dominion over the fish of the sea, and over the birds of the air, and over the cattle, and over all the wild animals of the earth, and over every creeping thing that creeps upon the earth.' So God created humankind in his image, in the image of God he created them; male and female he created them.

Image-making is a feature of our society. Publicists influence the way in which the media present famous people. Advertisers help firms to create an aura around their products. Most of us take trouble at times to create a good impression.

This is God's project, too—image-making, shaping human life to be like God, expressing his own character in and through people of flesh and blood. Our own images may be selective or even deceitful in intent, but God's image-making is true, wholesome and 'very good' (1:31). To be made in God's image is a basic aspect of our being, a truth at the root of all human life.

Image implies shared responsibility, 'dominion over' the life of Earth. Men and women have the honour of representing God in this world. God has made creation beautiful and we can respond to that beauty and enjoy it with God. The world is rich and God invites us to live from its goodness. 'Dominion' is both dignity and delight, but alongside dignity and delight there is duty. We are tenants, caretakers, stewards. Holidaymakers may be able to walk away, confident that someone else will do the cleaning. Long-term tenants must keep the property in which they are living in good repair. Looking after God's world, treating its resources with care, is a gesture of respect to the one who designed and owns it.

Having authority involves being under authority, too. Humanity's role on earth, our power to use the planet to meet our needs, is a holy gift resulting from the creative generosity of God. We cannot use that power well unless we also respect the love that gave it to us in the first place. Are we concerned about our image? God is, too. Does our living reflect and display his image, his pattern and purpose in us?

Prayer

Lord, you entrust us with much and expect much from us. Teach us wisdom and care as we live in your world.

JP

Freedom to obey

Then God spoke all these words: I am the Lord your God, who brought you out of the land of Egypt, out of the house of slavery; you shall have no other gods before me.

Yesterday's reading from Genesis spoke of human life as it came from the maker's hand. The authority and duty of bearing God's image belongs to all the peoples of the world. Today's reading takes us forward to a different era and perspective, to the calling and shaping of a holy nation. The Ten Commandments emerge from Israel's relationship with God. Some of them express values that are honoured in many cultures. Yet, they have a special claim on the people of the Jewish and Christian traditions.

The Ten Commandments tell of God's authority to direct and describe human behaviour. God asks for commitment, but first God makes a commitment. He liberates, leads and loves his people, taking them out of slavery and along the road to freedom. God rescues and the people respond. The New Testament counterpart of this is found in 1 John 4:10, 19—we love because God first loved us, with a love that is shown in the cross of Christ.

'No other gods' means no divided loyalties, no hedging of bets, no discreet offerings to other deities as an insurance policy, just in case they turn out to be more real than the Lord. In some parts of today's world, the presence and claims of other gods are both obvious and tempting, but, wherever we are, this command puts our values, desires and ambitions to the test. What do we really want from life? Do we want to honour God above all else? Will our other commitments fit within that greater loyalty?

These commandments restrict in order to liberate. As the Highway Code limits how we drive, so it releases us to use our cars in safety. The lines on a sports field free the players to enjoy the game. The score of a musical composition liberates the orchestra to draw the best from each other. To put God first, and so commit ourselves to honouring all God's commandments, will release us to handle properly the freedom and responsibility God gives.

Prayer
May God teach us the limits and liberty of faithful obedience.

JP

Charisma and courage

Deborah, a prophetess... used to sit under the palm of Deborah between Ramah and Bethel in the hill country of Ephraim; and the Israelites came up to her for judgment. She sent and summoned Barak... and said to him, 'The Lord, the God of Israel, commands you, "Go, take position at Mount Tabor... I will draw out Sisera... with his chariots and his troops; and I will give him into your hand."' Barak said to her, 'If you will go with me, I will go...'

When the Israelites were putting down roots in the promised land, they had to ward off some hostile neighbours. A succession of leaders emerged, known as judges, often as God's gift for a period of threat or fear. Deborah was one of them—in fact, both a judge and a prophet.

Few of the prophets of Israel were women and few appear as early as the time of Judges. Yet, in Deborah, we see the authority of a true prophet at work and patterns of vocation that appear throughout the Old Testament.

Prophets cared about justice in their community. Some had to exercise a ministry of protest, to stand for truth and right in chaotic or careless times, but Deborah had a different role. People trusted her to rule and arbitrate disputes among her people.

A prophet's gift and calling were not usually a matter of office or ordination. Strength of character and relationship with God counted more than popularity or formal approval.

We cannot tell where Deborah's calling came from, but it was not common for a woman to take such a prominent and public role. Unusual abilities and wisdom must have marked her out. She was a woman of charisma, gifted by God.

Prophets would often bring God's word to a moment of crisis or opportunity. Whether by spiritual inspiration or clear-eyed observation or a combination of the two, Deborah spotted God's moment. Now was the time to drive out the foreign army. She spoke with conviction and eventually managed to drag Barak into action. Typically for the Old Testament, the prophet who lives close to God is more of a leader than the person who appears to be in charge. Authority does not always come neatly or conventionally wrapped.

Prayer

Give your people ears, O God, for your strange and searching word.

JP

Just the job

Give the king your justice, O God, and your righteousness to a king's son. May he judge your people with righteousness, and your poor with justice. May the mountains yield prosperity for the people, and the hills, in righteousness.

This psalm is a job description for Israel's king. Here are tasks for him to perform, standards to meet and a description of the effects that wise rule should have on a nation. The title links the psalm to Solomon's reign, when Israel was united and strong. To read and use the psalm in later generations, as Hebrew and Christian people have done, is to remember and hope that the best of the past may shape the future, that the ideals of one nation may inform the world.

Justice and righteousness are the main themes—a commitment to treat people fairly in court and law, and a concern for neighbourly and honest dealing in every sphere of life. These are hard values for any government to deliver. Complexity and compromise wait to ambush even the most decent and determined politician. So this psalm is a prayer. True justice and righteousness must be gifts of God. Even the best leaders need help if they are to manage public affairs well.

The poor will always be there (Deuteronomy 15:11), the easiest group to overlook, and therefore the people to think of first. The scales of law must not treat them as lightweights. Fairness often involves listening most carefully to the people with the quietest voices.

Then, says the psalm, the mountains and hills will deliver prosperity, the all-round goodness, security and peace of the Hebrew 'shalom'. A healthy economy and the proper use of nature's riches depend on people who can trust and honour their leaders and each other.

Solomon never fully matched this job description. Indeed, it bursts the limits of human possibility and points to God's greater kingdom. The hymn 'Hail to the Lord's Anointed' by Isaac Watts applies the whole psalm to Jesus and to his coming rule over the whole world. However, even a target that earth's rulers can never fully reach may still be a standard to challenge and guide them.

Prayer
'Pray for all in high positions, that we may be godly and quietly governed.' (1 Timothy 2:1–2)

JP

Middle-men for God

We obligate ourselves to bring the first fruits of our soil and the first fruits of all fruit of every tree, year by year, to the house of the Lord; also to bring to... the priests who minister in the house of our God, the firstborn of our sons and of our livestock, as it is written in the law, and the firstlings of our herds and of our flocks.

Many an Old Testament text shows one aspect or another of the work of Israel's priests. The book of Nehemiah is an account of rebuilding after exile and despair. There were city walls to raise, patterns of national life to restore and people who longed to recover spirit and hope. As confidence returns, we hear of the priestly ministry at the centre of the regular religious life of the temple and nation.

Chapters 8—10 tell of the public reading of Israel's Law and the people's confession and recommitment. The verses above reflect a resolve to live all of life in relation to God. The rhythms of season and soil, the new life of fruit and family and flock, are honoured as gifts of God. Portions of the crop are brought back as an offering, first-born sons are dedicated (Luke 2:22–24), first-born sheep and cattle are offered in sacrifice by the priests.

The priests' ministry was pastoral, concerned with sustaining the people's religious life as the heart of their whole life. Priests taught (Malachi 2:7) and offered

sacrifices, cared for the temple and its worship and even interpreted health regulations (Mark 1:44). This was a permanent task, handed down within families. Above all, it was an in-between role, one of mediation, representing the prayers and faith of the people before God and the presence of God among the people.

Mediation is a demanding role, bearing expectations from both sides. It may carry the spiritual authority of work done consistently and well, but there is no easy power. The priesthood of Jesus, his mediation, led to a cross. Christian leadership in any age brings holy burdens—the duty of praying for people, need for sympathy, insight and patience, the call to a consistently godly life.

Prayer

*Give thanks for those who mediate—
as their daily work, in their
families and among friends,
in faithful praying.*

JP

Dreaming in the dark

As I watched in the night visions, I saw one like a human being coming with the clouds of heaven. And he came to the Ancient One and was presented before him. To him was given dominion, glory and kingship, that all peoples, nations and languages should serve him. His dominion is an everlasting dominion that shall not pass away, and his kingship is one that shall never be destroyed.

Dreams may, by their very oddness, distort reality or distract us from it. The strangeness of some biblical dreams actually gives a new angle on life, takes away the limits of earthly perspective and suddenly discloses more of the wide purpose of God.

Daniel's 'night vision' speaks to an era in history when the Hebrew people were pressed by one empire after another. The early verses of Chapter 7 picture these empires as four fierce beasts. Finally, a fragile human figure comes into view—a 'son of man' as older translations say. God welcomes and honours him, and gives him authority and power. The empires cease to rage and he comes to reign.

This figure is a symbol of God's purpose in his chosen people. Amid the battering of history, Israel lived within God's greater story. She was a survivor, and one day she would bless the whole world with the reality of her God. The 'son of man' stood for her life, pictured in the authority given to a vulnerable human figure. He is earthly, yet in tune with the life of heaven. He comes as a person alone, but reaching wide and deep into the world's life. He is surely a symbol of hope to come.

The great reality lies both within the dream, and beyond the dream—suffering and sorrow will end and a new dawn will arrive. One who carries Israel's heritage and hope within himself, the great Son of man, will come. His authority will stretch across the world and in his name many nations will honour Israel's God. Daniel's night vision prepares for a coming day—that of Jesus Christ. For God works powerfully, but in odd ways—through dreams, signs and symbols and a carpenter on a cross.

Reflection

What helps you to 'dream for God', see beyond the experience of each day to the deeper purposes of God that run through your life?

JP

Who do you think you are?

The chief priests, the scribes and the elders came to him [Jesus] and said, 'By what authority are you doing these things? Who gave you this authority to do them?' Jesus said to them, 'I will ask you one question; answer me, and I will tell you by what authority I do these things. Did the baptism of John come from heaven, or was it of human origin? Answer me.'

Mark's Gospel is full of authority. The Son of Man has come and God is at work in him. Jesus teaches with a decisive note of power, driving out evil (1:22, 27). He has the authority to forgive, challenge the conventions of the Law and send apostles out in power (2:10; 3:4, 14–15).

This authority was recognized by those around Jesus, but it came from within—from his closeness to God, from the Spirit's touch on his life. He spoke of the greatness of a servant lifestyle in contrast to the strutting and harshness of Gentile rulers (10:41–45). He ministered as one poor, humble and homeless, and this simplicity carried a conviction of its own.

Eventually the religious leaders ask, 'By what authority?' They ask about his cleansing of the temple, but the question seems to reach further. Who is he and by what right does he act? The reader already knows, so the question seems perverse and almost pointless, but Jesus' answer is awkward too. 'You answer my question, then I'll answer yours.' Is he just sliding out of a difficult conversation?

I think he meant that his authority was like John the Baptist's—the authority of prayer, poverty and direct preaching. People who respected John the waymaker would also respond to Jesus, of whom John spoke. Those who wavered, who found the directness of John's message unsettling, would find some objection to Jesus' ministry, too.

Jesus' authority in people's lives today comes from our relationship with him, from the conviction that his person and his Spirit are within us. Perhaps we, too, will not understand him properly unless we listen to the needs and challenges near to home. Who is your John the Baptist, the person who helps you to take Jesus seriously?

Sunday prayer

Spirit of God, prepare the way of the Lord in our hearts and lives. In the wilderness of our living, make a straight path for Jesus.

JP

Blood and bluster

When his [Herod's] daughter... came in and danced, she pleased Herod and his guests; and the king said to the girl, 'Ask me for whatever you wish, and I will give it.' And he solemnly swore to her, 'Whatever you ask me, I will give you, even half of my kingdom.' She went out and said to her mother, 'What should I ask for?' She replied, 'The head of John the baptizer.'

Herod Antipas was not really a king. His proper title was Tetrarch, the ruler of a quarter. His father's lands had been divided and his share included Galilee and the east bank of Jordan. In the Gospels and in wider history, he gives an impression of insecurity, handling rather erratically the limited responsibility that had fallen to him.

In this sad passage, Herod's royal authority is both absolute—he can apparently do what he likes on his own territory—and oddly pathetic. He is a prisoner of a girl's dance, foolish words, drink, his wife's cunning, the desire to impress, his position as king among guests. Character, dignity, decency seem not to influence the course of events. He is 'deeply grieved' by the corner into which he has painted himself (6:26). However, this is not the sort of 'godly grief' that makes a difference to behaviour (see 2 Corinthians 7:10).

The sense of authority abused, of harsh and shallow power, stands out very clearly in Mark's story. A few verses earlier, the disciples go out with authority to heal (6:7, 13). A few verses later, Jesus presides over a simple yet generous banquet (6:41). By contrast, Herod's power is used to harm and kill and his grand dinner party turns into a grim and sordid gathering.

Herod Antipas wanted to be respected, but you cannot win respect by bluster. Even when our responsibilities do not match our hopes or ambitions, we can at least try to manage them with honour and care.

We can only wonder what the 'leaders of Galilee' (6:21) made of this episode. They will have had little stomach for their dessert afterwards. Some of life's invitations and occasions are neither worthy nor pleasant and we would do better to avoid them.

Reflection

'When you eat with an important person, be careful' (Proverbs 23:1).

JP

Man on trial

Pilate therefore said to him [Jesus], 'Do you refuse to speak to me? Do you not know that I have power to release you, and power to crucify you?' Jesus answered him, 'You would have no power over me unless it had been given you from above; therefore the one who handed me over to you is guilty of a greater sin.' From then on Pilate tried to release him, but the Jews cried out, 'If you release this man you are no friend of the emperor. Everyone who claims to be a king sets himself against the emperor.'

Pontius Pilate was Prefect of Judea from AD26 to 36, the chief local official of the Roman Empire, and responsible for order. He appears to have had little sympathy or sensitivity for the people he ruled. He neither understood Jewish life and culture very well, nor had a sure touch in tense situations. The trial of Jesus presents him as a man out of his depth.

Pilate has complete power to decide Jesus' guilt or innocence and pass sentence, but he cannot decide. He tries to draw Jesus into discussion, but Jesus has had enough. He reminds Pilate that his official power comes from God. So, Pilate cannot help being in this tricky situation as God has allowed him this authority and now other people are trying to exploit his position.

Verse 12 shows Pilate in an awkward bind. The word 'Jews' in John's Gospel does not mean all Jewish people—it might be better translated as 'Judeans', referring to the aristocratic Jerusalem leaders. These men are shrewd and subtle. They suggest to Pilate that they are better loyalists than he is. Here is a prisoner who claims to be a king. They have arrested him. Now, if Pilate does not execute him, then perhaps Pilate is not committed enough to his own king, the Roman emperor.

People who carry authority often handle it better than Pilate did. His story highlights two important factors in using power responsibly—care in understanding people and courage not to be pushed into making bad decisions.

Prayer

Pray for people around you who need care and courage to handle their responsibilities in local and national government, police, prison and probation officers, doctors and nurses, teachers and parents.

JP

On trust

Therefore, since it is by God's mercy that we are engaged in this ministry, we do not lose heart. We have renounced the shameful things that one hides; we refuse to practise cunning or to falsify God's word; but by the open statement of the truth we commend ourselves to the conscience of everyone in the sight of God... For we do not proclaim ourselves; we proclaim Jesus Christ as Lord and ourselves as your slaves for Jesus' sake.

Many passages in Paul's letters reflect his authority as an apostle—his sense of being sent by God, his care and commitment to the churches he founded, his passion to see these young Christians tackling faith and life in the right way. Sometimes his approach and language are quite strong, but these verses from 2 Corinthians have a very different tone.

Paul's relationship with this church has run into serious trouble. Some visitors to Corinth have persuaded the Christians there not to trust him, so Paul has his back to the wall. We find him here, not using the weight of his apostolic clout, but explaining his ministry. The authority in what he does is a matter not just of source, but also of substance—the way that he follows and obeys God's call.

So Paul writes about commitment, integrity and sincere and direct speech. Elsewhere he calls himself a 'steward' (1 Corinthians 4:1). He treats the Christian message in the way that a responsible servant handles the master's property—he is mindful of the owner's rights, reputation and purpose. To the church, he calls himself and his companions 'your slaves'. A Christian preacher has no private agenda, no hidden plans for personal advancement, but offers all available energy to the church's good.

Where is the authority in all that? In three places—the message, the manner and the master. The word preached, and the honesty and personal humility with which it is preached, will draw attention to God, whose work and word they are. Even in the Church, we sometimes give more attention to show than substance, but the people with deep, lasting influence will be those with substance to their living.

Prayer

May God help us to serve humbly, speak honestly and live by trust and truth.

JP

Listening to the Spirit

Then the apostles and the elders, with the consent of the whole church, decided to choose men from among their members, and to send them to Antioch with Paul and Barnabas... with the following letter: 'The brothers, both the apostles and the elders, to the believers of Gentile origin in Antioch and Syria and Cilicia, greetings. Since we have heard that certain persons... have said things to disturb you... we have decided unanimously to choose representatives and send them to you... For it has seemed good to the Holy Spirit and to us to impose on you no further burden than these essentials...'

Most churches use councils in some form. Christians meet to try to discern God's way, and to agree Church policy and plans. How councils operate varies widely. Many Christians see in Acts 15, in the Council of Jerusalem, an early example of this sort of meeting. It exercised authority and helped to resolve a problem in the churches. The issue was new converts—how to bring them into fellowship and what sort of lifestyle to expect of them. Our concern today is the way in which the meeting worked.

Commitment: this was a family gathering. You can choose your friends, but you must live within the family God gives you. It's the same in our spiritual lives. There was a sense of belonging together, of mutual care and concern. Christians are brothers and sisters, a family in faith (Romans 12:5).

Consultation: that family commitment meant that different opinions had to be thoughtfully considered. There had been a long debate (15:2). Authority, solid decision, often depends on attentive listening and minds coming gradually to a shared insight. To reach the point of saying, 'It seemed good to the Holy Spirit and to us' may take time. The Holy Spirit is patient enough to handle this, if we are, too.

Communication: the decision was communicated in the visible form of a letter and the love and pastoral interest of trusted messengers. It may require both paper and people to make a decision clear and credible to those affected by it.

Reflection

Christian decision-making involves finding what seems good to the Holy Spirit, and following that way with our own commitment and action. Which of the two, in your experience, is harder?

JP

Powers that be

Let every person be subject to the governing authorities; for there is no authority except from God, and those authorities that exist have been instituted by God... Do you wish to have no fear of the authority? Then do what is good, and you will receive its approval... For the same reason you also pay taxes, for the authorities are God's servants... Pay to all what is due to them—taxes... revenue... respect.

Paul wrote the letters gathered together in Romans to a fragile and vulnerable Christian fellowship. As he writes, there is grumbling unrest in Rome over levels of tax and Paul warns the Christians not to get sucked in. This would be a needless and damaging quarrel. Government has its proper purposes—preventing and punishing wrong and protecting and promoting what is good. Christians can support that work by paying taxes. They should respect government and 'must be subject' by maintaining good conduct.

Some Christians are uneasy about this passage. It seems to put all governments, even those marked by muddle or malice, out of range of legitimate criticism. Can that be right? Other Christian thinkers have found this a liberating text. If we can trust the state, because God put it there, then the Church can press on confidently with spiritual concerns, knowing that secular affairs are in good hands.

Perhaps the best interpretation lies between these two views. Government, as an aspect of life, is a gift of God, but Romans 13 gives governments a standard to live up to—a reminder of why they are there. Do they use their powers to deter evil? Do they spend the people's taxes to foster and praise good conduct? When they do, we thank God for them.

We always owe rulers our prayers (1 Timothy 2:1–2). At times, we may owe them our questions too (Psalm 82:2–4). If a government blatantly fails to deliver, Christians will not be comfortably silent. Many of us, who live under stable rule, should thank God for the privilege of being governed. So far as we conscientiously can, we offer our submission and support—even as we pursue the deeper Christian duty of love (Romans 13:8).

Prayer

Thank God for all that is upright and true in your nation's government. Pray that goodness will flourish in your land.

JP

Thou art worthy

Then one of the elders said to me, 'Do not weep. See, the Lion of the tribe of Judah, the Root of David, has conquered, so that he can open the scroll and its seven seals.' Then I saw between the throne and the four living creatures and among the elders a Lamb standing as if it had been slaughtered.

Yesterday's reading spoke of the proper purposes of state and governmental power. Revelation addresses a situation where the Roman Empire has claimed too much power for itself. The seven churches of Asia Minor (western Turkey) were surrounded by images and temples. The empire invited the worship of colonial people, as if the emperor himself were a god. Even something basically good—rule, order, government—can be distorted and diverted into something ugly and false.

The visions of Revelation debunk and unmask the myth of imperial glory, by putting in its place a truer and more lasting picture of worship and power. Chapters 4 and 5 are the threshold of the main part of the book. The foundation they lay is a grand view of worship. Chapter 4 shows the throne of God, surrounded by the praise of heaven, the worship of the Church and the sound, light and life of creation. Grandeur, glory and greatness are there. God deserves honour and praise. There is none to compare with him.

Then the Lamb steps forward, marked with wounds of slaughter, the image and presence of the crucified Jesus. He comes to receive worship with God, to open the scroll that holds the future, to be hailed as 'Lion of Judah'. True authority for heaven to praise, the power to shape the life and history of Earth, comes from the cross.

When government goes awry, the Church may rejoice that lasting authority lies not with states and rulers, but with God and the Lamb. Suffering love, patient reconciliation, costly commitment and lowly service are the victories and values that will endure. We are beckoned by the cross to serve in its light and live by its love, whether the world counts us strong or weak, powerful or foolish.

Prayer

'To the one seated on the throne and to the Lamb be blessing and honour and glory and might for ever and ever!' (Revelation 5:13)

JP

Slaves of our own 'freedom'?

This is the reason that I Paul am a prisoner for Christ Jesus for the sake of you Gentiles—for surely you have already heard of the commission of God's grace that was given to me for you, and how the mystery was made known to me by revelation, as I wrote above in a few words, a reading of which will enable you to perceive my understanding of the mystery of Christ.

Prison bars come in infinite varieties. And freedom isn't always what it seems. In today's reading we find Paul speaking from a place of imprisonment, yet proclaiming the very gateway of freedom.

Fresh in my memory is a close encounter with the Statue of Liberty, which has welcomed so many immigrants, seeking a new life in the 'promised land' of the New World, and which still holds the flame of freedom high against the Manhattan skyline. The streets of Manhattan, however, along with so many other city streets throughout the world, tell a different story—a story of enslavement to the compulsions of consumerism and the desperate human need for a sense of meaning and self-worth. Behind all our brave assertions of a 'free world' lies a new kind of totalitarianism that first fills us with fear of our own inadequacy and then sells us the means to make ourselves 'worthy', thereby plunging us ever deeper into debt and despair.

Paul, behind his prison bars, knows a different story, one that begins by enfolding us in God's unconditional love, whatever the shape of our bodies or the state of our minds, and goes on not only to free us from the darkness we have created for ourselves, but to recreate us in the image of our creator. This is a freedom that no credit card can purchase. Its power doesn't falter when the money markets crash, nor does its light fail in our most abject darkness. It is the light of love that once blinded Paul and now sets us free from the darkness of our fears.

Sunday reflection

We value our liberty so highly that we are prepared to spill each other's blood in its defence. Genuine freedom carries a different price tag and only one man's blood was shed to restore it to us.

MS

A local story becomes universal

In former generations this mystery was not made known to humankind, as it has now been revealed to his holy apostles and prophets by the Spirit: that is, the Gentiles have become fellow-heirs, members of the same body, and sharers in the promise in Jesus Christ through the gospel.

We are often told that we live in a 'global village', easily interconnected by the news media, Internet and international travel. We live in an age that has shown us our own planet home from outer space and revealed that we are one family, living on the third rock from the sun, destined to journey together, for better or for worse. In our time, this mystery of being 'members of the same body' has been revealed to us in a very new way.

For Paul, there was an even more profound sense of a new vision of the earth and its human family. Once enlightened by the light of Christ, it became obvious to him that such a vision could not be limited to just one people. The Gentiles were as much a part of this new kingdom of light as were the people of Israel. The good news was for everybody.

In this way, the local story becomes the global story. The tribal history of one people becomes the universal mystery of all peoples. Like the ripples created when a pebble is thrown into a pool, our understanding of the limitlessness of God's love expands in every new generation until it encompasses the whole of creation.

Perhaps the kingdom of God can be compared to a global village, too. It grows in every new age from the seeds planted in local soil, in the hearts of individuals whose lives have been touched in some personal way by the fire of the gospel, and it expands like those ripples on the pool, until it encompasses all life.

For such a vision, exclusiveness is never an option. If we try to fence off our own sections of the kingdom, we are regressing to a blinkered outlook, which Paul is challenging in today's reading.

Reflection

Jesus' arms, outstretched on the cross, are the measure of the kingdom of God's love. If we seek to limit his inclusiveness, we are crucifying him anew.

MS

A good servant

Of this gospel I have become a servant according to the gift of God's grace that was given to me by the working of his power.

What might it mean to be a 'servant of the gospel'?

Some 'servants' are more helpful than others. We have all encountered those personal assistants whose role in life seems to be preventing anyone getting to their employer rather than enabling access. We have also come across one of that small minority of doctors' receptionists who so terrify us with their intimidating presence that we think twice before going to see the doctor at all. What about those 'helpful' menu systems that change a simple telephone call into an obstacle course of options before we finally reach a real person? These so-called 'servants' are actually obstructions. God forbid that we should be like this when we share the good news. So what makes a good servant?

Well, Paul was one and so was John the Baptist, to mention just two examples. Their lives and ministry show us that to serve the gospel is to make ourselves transparent, so that others might see Christ through us or, rather, that others should see through us to the Christ beyond us (and above, below, around and within us).

Such people are like icons.

An icon is a means to deep prayer. It is painted as a result of prayer, in such a way that it draws the praying person through and beyond it, offering a kind of gateway to God. An idol, on the other hand, is something that traps our attention and fixes it on itself so that we never get beyond it to God. We are called to let our lives be icons—revealing God's presence, never focusing on any lesser reality.

So, are we really serving the gospel in all we do and all we are or are we serving some lesser reality, such as our own church or denomination or our own subtly disguised desire for status, all of which can block the passage to God for others?

Reflection

The most effective windows are made of clear glass. The most effective servants of the gospel are those least cluttered with their own image and agenda.

MS

62

Boundless life from tiny seeds

Although I am the very least of all the saints, this grace was given to me to bring to the Gentiles the news of the boundless riches of Christ, and to make everyone see what is the plan of the mystery hidden for ages in God who created all things; so that through the church the wisdom of God in its rich variety might now be made known to the rulers and authorities in the heavenly places.

The Greek philosopher Empedocles once described God as 'a circle whose centre is everywhere and whose circumference is nowhere'. In other words, there is something of the living reality of God implanted in the heart of every one of God's creatures. This is the God whose centre is everywhere—in you and in everyone you will meet today—but the circumference of the circle of God's presence is nowhere because God is without limit.

This is surely part of what Paul means by 'the mystery hidden for ages in God' (v. 9), which, thanks to Paul's ministry, is now being revealed to the entire world.

For us today, it is impossible to imagine the idea of keeping the mystery of God contained in one small part of the earth. What is much harder to take on board is the fact that a kernel of this immense mystery is present in our own human hearts, by the grace of God. This tiny kernel of God's infinite presence will grow and flourish and bear fruit, if we allow it to.

If Paul considers himself to be 'the very least of all the saints' (v. 8), what should we say of ourselves? Yet, that tiny particle of God-aliveness in our hearts has the potential to reveal a unique aspect of God's kingdom. The tiny seed, as Jesus tells us himself, can grow into a tree that provides space in which the birds can build their nests (Matthew 13:31–32). In this way, we are called to participate in the coming to be of the 'boundless riches of Christ' while never losing the awed awareness that the mystery of God is at once for ever beyond our human thinking and imagining, yet accessible to us by the power of God's Son.

Reflection

Even the least among us is a bearer of God's presence and a seed of God's kingdom on earth.

MS

A golden thread

This was in accordance with the eternal purpose that he has carried out in Christ Jesus our Lord, in whom we have access to God in boldness and confidence through faith in him. I pray therefore that you may not lose heart over my sufferings for you; they are your glory.

An old folk story tells about a little girl who once wandered through a dark forest and came upon an ancient castle deep in the heart of the woods. Tentatively, she climbed up to the attic, where she found an old lady spinning golden thread. The old lady welcomed the child and gave her a golden ring, and told her, 'I am constantly here for you, spinning the golden thread of Life. Wear this ring always. It joins you to the thread of life, which can never be broken. That thread connects you eternally to me, and I love you unconditionally and will always hold you close to my heart.'

The child was delighted to have the golden ring, but dismayed to discover that the golden thread itself was invisible. She was going to have to trust that what the old lady had told her was true, for she couldn't see the thread that connected her to the golden spool of life.

It can sometimes feel like that in our Christian living. We know that we are eternally connected to God, but we can't actually see the thread! We may lose heart, as surely the first Christians may have done as they faced the hardships of living by faith alone.

Today, Paul reminds us that, through the gospel, we do have real, embodied and unfailing access to God. Jesus is what makes the invisible thread real. We can live in bold confidence that this is the thread that can never be severed, not even by our own sinfulness.

Reflection

The ways of life can be dark and winding, but the gospel gives us a golden thread in the life of Jesus. Take a moment tonight to look back over your day, just noticing any incidents that come to mind. How would Jesus have responded to these incidents? Tell him how you feel about how you responded yourself.

MS

Whose name?

For this reason I bow my knees before the Father, from whom every family in heaven and on earth takes its name.

When a child is conceived, it becomes a new person in whom the seed of the parent becomes incarnate. That seed grows and becomes in turn a carrier of life for new generations. We take our names from those who first gave us our physical life. In these verses, Paul takes this logic of life much further, reminding us that the spiritual—and eternal—life that we carry has been conceived in us by God, the author of all life. We carry this seed of God within us, allowing it to grow to maturity in our everyday relationships and choices. We carry, spiritually, the name of the God who gives our souls birth and continuance.

In the face of this awesome fact, Paul falls to his knees in wonder as he reflects on the fact that every single person who has lived on earth, lives now on earth, or ever will live on earth, is part of the blossoming forth of this first seed of life.

We are not simply individual carriers of God's eternal life. We are in relationship. To be is to be in relationship. It is almost impossible for a human being to survive, and remain sane, for very long in solitary confinement. We are intimately interrelated and express this sense of interdependency in our image of God as Trinitarian—a relational God.

Just as each of us takes our spiritual name from the one who called us into the new birth of faith, so each of our communities —whether family, circles of friends or faith communities—is called to reflect the circle of love that flows eternally through the persons of the Trinity. God is a circuit of energy and power and, in him, all things become possible—but only if we allow ourselves to be channels of that loving energy and not contain it for our own private purposes.

Reflection

Whatever I keep for myself and mark with my own name dies with me. Whatever I share with the community of all creation, for the glory of God's name, lives on, from generation to generation, carrying God's love all down the ages.

MS

Rooted and grounded

I pray that, according to the riches of his glory, he may grant that you may be strengthened in your inner being with power through his Spirit, and that Christ may dwell in your hearts through faith, as you are being rooted and grounded in love.

When I was a child, we lived close to a bluebell wood. April was always my favourite month because, at that time, the woods were carpeted with perfect blue and fresh spring green. It seemed to me like the nearest thing to heaven.

Inevitably, I tried gathering the bluebells, putting them in a vase to decorate my bedroom or to give to my parents. Just as inevitably, after a few hours the bluebells drooped, wilted and died. I soon learned the lesson that things grow best when they are—as Paul puts it in today's reading—'rooted and grounded' (v. 17). In fact, if they are not rooted and grounded, they will surely die.

In later life, I have sometimes rejoiced over a bunch of tulips in the springtime. I have placed them carefully and lovingly in a vase, only to see them bend themselves over in despair, desperate for their former habitat. However, there is hope for prostrate tulips. I have found that fresh water gives them new life. I have even watched as they quite literally rose up again in front of my eyes, drawing deeply on the life-giving water.

What is true for bluebells and tulips is just as true for each of us. We cannot grow spiritually unless we are rooted and grounded in God and God's word. When Christ does indeed dwell in our hearts, then his presence and power literally rises up through us, strengthening our inner being, just as fresh water gives new life to the flowers.

Resurrection like this becomes a moment-by-moment possibility. All that is needed is for us to acknowledge our deep need of God's life-giving water. God will do the rest.

Reflection

Take time today, especially if you feel drained of energy, to dip your heart into the fresh spring of God's love in a moment of silent prayer. Let God's Spirit rise up in you anew.

MS

The snapshot and the real thing

I pray that you may have the power to comprehend, with all the saints, what is the breadth and length and height and depth, and to know the love of Christ that surpasses knowledge, so that you may be filled with all the fullness of God.

It's the beginning of the summer holiday season. Time for postcards from friends in faraway places—or maybe a picture of a local scene, reminding us of how beautiful our own homeland can be when seen through holiday eyes.

Maybe you are planning your own holidays, browsing through the brochures. They will tell you rather more about the potential destination than a mere postcard. They will reveal how to get there, where to stay and how much it's all going to cost, but there is no substitute for the real experience! To actually be in the place, meet the people who live there, taste the food, smell the mountain breezes or the salt sea spray, let the weather bathe us in sunshine or soak us with rain—this is to begin to know a place and its people, and its subtle and unique atmosphere.

Perhaps Paul is saying something similar in today's Bible reading. We can learn something about the love of Christ just from the say-so of other people—a kind of 'postcard' understanding—just a snapshot image of God's mystery, chosen and communicated to us by someone else. Often, such a snapshot can whet our appetites and we should not hesitate to send each other this kind of 'postcard', sharing in some way, however inadequate, the good news of God's all-embracing love.

We can gain deeper understanding from the 'brochures'—especially from scripture—but the only way to begin to know the breadth and length, the height and depth of this mystery is to live it ourselves. We can do as Paul invites us to do today—open ourselves to the fullness of God, which is both hidden in, and revealed by, everything around us.

Sunday reflection

To focus on ourselves is to narrow our perspective to a pinhole view of life. To focus on God and God's creation, God's world and our fellow creatures, is to become aware of the infinite dimensions of God's loving presence.

MS

A bubble in God's ocean

Now to him who by the power at work within us is able to accomplish abundantly far more than all we can ask or imagine, to him be glory in the church and in Christ Jesus to all generations, for ever and ever. Amen

The imagination is one of our most powerful human gifts. To be able to imagine what is not yet present, or even possible, is to stand on the threshold of discovery. Without imagination we would probably never venture beyond our own front door. We would assume, in computer parlance, that 'what you see is what you get'. Our lives would be flat and boring.

With the help of our imagination, we can fly to the stars and probe the many universes of all that might yet be. We can speculate on better ways in which we can be human beings, new approaches to healing our hurts, teaching our young, making a more just world. What we have once imagined can, in the course of time, become real. We have the potential to make our dreams come true. Yet, here is Paul, telling us that the power of God, working within us, can accomplish abundantly more than anything we could ever imagine! Our human brains imagine much but simply don't deal in those dimensions.

I often apologize for my own 'senior moments' with the remark 'I have the attention span of a goldfish'. Of course I don't really mean it, but, if I am honest, my own imagination and power of thought are little more remarkable than the intellect of a goldfish when compared with the power of God.

Comparisons are meaningless, of course. What matters here is not to measure ourselves against each other or against any other creature, let alone against God. What matters is that we open ourselves to that amazing power that flows with redeeming love through the gospel story, through our hearts and through our world—a power that surpasses our wildest hopes and dreams.

Reflection

The sphere of our own understanding is a mere bubble in the ocean of our ever-present God. It can reflect, but never contain, the reality of the kingdom. Yet, in the heart of that little bubble, lies the God-given power to journey in faith far beyond our own small ego-world, carried by the One who holds the universe in being.

MS

Rock into pebbles

I therefore, the prisoner in the Lord, beg you to lead a life worthy of the calling to which you have been called, with all humility and gentleness, with patience, bearing with one another in love, making every effort to maintain the unity of the Spirit in the bond of peace.

A nun once told me that she had been helped in community life by imagining all the sisters who lived in her convent as a bag of stones—many different shapes and sizes and, initially at least, all rather rough-edged and sharp. In the community 'bag', they jostled into one another and life could be very painful. However, over time, the jostling and clashing had an unexpected result—it polished the irregular stones into smooth pebbles, each with her own beauty and then much less prone to jar the others with her presence.

Well, it isn't always so easy—as the nun I spoke with would have been the first to confirm. The worst tensions in life are usually with those closest to us. Maybe it's because they're the ones with the greatest power to hurt us, and the ones who make the most demands on us. It would seem so much easier to just move off into seclusion and avoid the friction.

Paul doesn't give us that option and nor does God. God is a relational God—the three-in-one Trinity—an icon of our own non-negotiable call to be in the right relationship with one another. We are urged today to 'bear with one another in love' (v. 2) and 'make every effort' to live in unity and peace. That's a big request! It's relatively easy to feel in harmony with those in distant lands. They are unlikely to knock on our door, asking for practical help. It's no problem to get on with strangers across the city. They're not the ones who criticize us and put us down. Relating harmoniously with our immediate family and colleagues is far, far harder.

Yet these cutting edges of our lives are the very place where the hard rock is being smoothed into pebbles. This, indeed, is the work of the Spirit.

Reflection

The most important human relationship in our lives may be with the person we find it hard—or even impossible—to get along with.

MS

EPHESIANS 4:4–6 (NRSV)

Called to be one

There is one body and one Spirit, just as you were called to the one hope of your calling, one Lord, one faith, one baptism, one God and Father of all, who is above all and through all and in all.

One! What is 'one'? 'One' is what there is before there are fractions. 'One' is about wholeness and unity—a unity that comes into being when the fractions are brought into the right relationship with each other—just as the three persons of God are in eternal loving inter-relationship.

Most human beings, of whatever culture, sense that we all come from a source in which we were 'one' and that to return to that deep source is also the destination of our living. The Genesis story confirms this intuition and names the source as God, from whom all creation springs.

The story of the evolution of our earth and its creatures, which reflects the gradual unfolding of the different species from that first source, reveals that life began in the primeval waters on the earth. As Christians, we believe that a deeper evolution is also taking place. This is the evolution of the kingdom of God and we are called to participate in this unfolding of God's mystery on earth. However, we cannot do this unless, and until, our fragmented hearts are restored to the wholeness that sin has shattered.

Our participation in the coming of the kingdom begins with water, too—the waters of baptism. It proceeds in the power of faith—our trust in the power of grace to restore us, the fractions, to the wholeness we have lost as a result of the breakdown of our relationships with God, with each other and with creation.

There is one Lord—the source of all that is. There is one faith, that trusts in the process of restoration due to the power of the death and resurrection of Christ. There is one baptism, drawing us deep into the waters of God's love, restoring our hearts to the right relationship with the heart of God so that our spiritual evolution may begin.

Reflection

God calls us to be one body—the body of Christ in our own time and place. Those whom God has thus joined with grace, let not man put asunder!

MS

At the bottom of the well

But each of us was given grace according to the measure of Christ's gift. Therefore it is said, 'When he ascended on high he made captivity itself a captive; he gave gifts to his people.' (When it says, 'He ascended', what does it mean but that he had also descended into the lower parts of the earth? He who descended is the same one who ascended far above all the heavens, so that he might fill all things.)

Life and circumstances, or simply our own entanglement in darkness, sometimes seem to drop us down into a deep, dark well. Something happens, perhaps, or something or someone we cherished is lost to us and, for a while, we see nothing but the black shaft of despair. We feel ourselves falling and dread the moment when our lives might crash against the rock.

Paul reminds us today that Jesus knows this dark shaft—that he himself descended to the depths of human experience. Because of this, the shaft, far from being a place of despair, has become, for us, a well of new hope and new life.

A well can look terrifying as we gaze into its dark depths, but it is also the source of living water. To reach that living water, we may have to risk the drop and feel the pain of hitting the rock. When this happens, we discover that the rock bottom is nothing other than the arms of God, inviting us to experience 'metanoia'—a Greek word meaning 'to turn around, go in a new direction'. At the bottom of the well, if we surrender to the power of grace, we do indeed find a turning-point. There, Christ gives us the living water we need and the strength and hope to return to life, renewed, refreshed and restored.

At the bottom of the well, God waits not only to fill the buckets of our hearts with living water but also full-fill all things.

Reflection

When we fly our kites or launch our rockets, we know that 'what goes up must come down'. Let us trust in the dynamic of grace, even in the darkest places of our experience, that 'what goes down will come up', if we can only trust the process that Jesus has opened up to us.

MS

Living cells in the body of Christ

The gifts he gave were that some would be apostles, some prophets, some evangelists, some pastors and teachers, to equip the saints for the work of ministry, for building up the body of Christ, until all of us come to the unity of the faith and of the knowledge of the Son of God, to maturity, to the measure of the full stature of Christ.

The body of Christ is a living, growing reality—the embodiment on earth of God's mystery and love. It is a reality in which we all participate. We are living cells in the body of Christ.

This is a mind-blowing fact. It means that each one of us carries something in the core of our being that identifies us as belonging to Christ, just as our physical DNA identifies each cell in our bodies as a part of the whole of who we are. It also means that each one of us has our own unique role to play in growing that body of Christ and maintaining its well-being.

Paul reminds us in today's reading that these various cells in the body have their own functions. When I think about the cells in my body, I don't find that the bone cells, for example, have a problem with not being muscle cells or that my fingernails start sulking because they are not teeth. Each cell does its own thing, but each cell's purpose is to build up and maintain the whole body. If any cells opt out of this contract, they damage the health of the whole. If they try to take over, they become cancerous.

When we apply this analogy, as Paul does here and elsewhere, to the Church, we can see that each one of us affects the whole people of God. To participate creatively in the building up of the body of Christ requires that we live true to who we really are—the person God created us, uniquely to be—and that we remain in constant and loving communion with each other.

Reflection

Each cell is God's gift to the whole body. In German, the word 'gift' means 'poison'. May the living cell that each of us is called to be bring life, not disease, to the whole body.

MS

Woven together in love

We must no longer be children, tossed to and fro and blown about by every wind of doctrine, by people's trickery, by their craftiness in deceitful scheming. But speaking the truth in love, we must grow up in every way into him who is the head, into Christ, from whom the whole body, joined and knit together by every ligament with which it is equipped, as each part is working properly, promotes the body's growth in building itself up in love.

Our ability to delude ourselves is phenomenal. This goes through everything we do, not only as individuals, but as families, as Church and in our nation states and global dealings.

At the surface of our lives, we are subject to constant change, at the mercy of every wind that blows and prey to every kind of deception. God calls us to go deeper than this to find the ground of our being. He calls us back to our roots, which are to be found in God. Only by living from these deep roots, and drawing our strength and inspiration from those roots, will we be empowered to grow into co-operating members of the body of Christ.

If we think of a tree, we see the branches above ground, often tossed by wind and rain, helpless to defend themselves from the rage of the elements. However, if we could go below ground, we would see a deep and complicated root system 'joined and knitted together' (v. 16), so interwoven that it becomes impossible to distinguish the roots of one tree from those of its neighbour. We, too, are interwoven with each other in the depths of our being that only God can see.

Whatever happens to the tree above ground—including its ability to grow and bear fruit—depends absolutely on this deep underground root system. This is the source of its nourishment and the basis of its stability. From these roots alone will it grow and flourish.

Reflection

The ground in which our lives are planted is nothing less than the immensity of God's love. As long as we live from this deeper level, rooted in the very mystery of God, then we will not be shaken, either by the deceptions of others or by our own self-deceptions.

MS

Hebrews 8—10

I have it on good authority that there is no particularly good basis for saying who actually wrote the epistle to the Hebrews. If you want to believe it was Paul, I don't suppose he or the actual writer of the letter will mind in the slightest any more. What we do know for sure is that the person who produced this original and creative piece of writing was passionately excited about the sheer greatness of Jesus Christ and the new life he has made possible for those who follow him. Using the Old Testament themes of priesthood and sacrifice, he sets out to explain how man-made means of achieving access to God have been replaced by the real thing. Jesus himself, because of his obedience in going to the cross, dying and rising again, has become our great high priest, defending and representing us to his Father. The writer invites us to grasp a new and deeper understanding of Jesus and the completeness of his triumph over death.

Chapters 8 to 10 are specifically concerned with Jesus' role as the only high priest necessary to our encounters with God, the fulfilment of Jeremiah's prophecy about God's Law being written on our hearts, the need to take hold of the absolute forgiveness offered by Jesus and the need to persevere and be courageous because the eventual rewards will be richer than we can possibly imagine.

This all sounds nice and neat and tidy, but the truth is that my own response to these chapters has been fairly ragged and emotional. The idea that there is a place where everything comes right and the real thing turns out to be infinitely better than its shadow or counterfeit, well, that is my yearning and my dream. There are times when I get so chronically weary of what we have come to perceive as Christianity and all its trappings. Human beings can't help it, I suppose. They just have to make up pictures and shapes and rhymes and patterns and mantras and all manner of religious bits and pieces. All this will fall away in the end, like those bits that drop off space rockets as they go higher and higher. I look forward to that. My little excursion into Hebrews has encouraged me to believe that the place we are heading for on that final journey might be exciting beyond belief. What do you think?

Adrian Plass

A copy and a shadow

The point of what we are saying is this: We do have such a high priest, who sat down at the right hand of the throne of the Majesty in heaven, and who serves in the sanctuary, the true tabernacle set up by the Lord, not by man. Every high priest is appointed to offer both gifts and sacrifices, and so it was necessary for this one also to have something to offer. If he were on earth, he would not be a priest, for there are already men who offer the gifts prescribed by the law. They serve at a sanctuary that is a copy and a shadow of what is in heaven...

A copy and a shadow, eh? Interesting.

For most of the early part of my life I had a not-very-rational idea that eventually I would come across a string that, when I pulled it, would oblige everything to fall into place and make sense. This was not, as far as I know, connected with any kind of spiritual need or instinct. It probably had more to do with the fact that I had experienced a tumultuous childhood at the same time as being a voracious reader of books. On the one side I saw chaos, on the other the sculpted quality of emotional order that literature was able to bring to life. Perhaps I vaguely assumed that this calmer construct of being was bound to become available to me one day in the future.

Whatever its origins, as the evidence against my ridiculously optimistic string-pulling theory attained mountainous heights, I abandoned it. Now, however, as I have more time in this world to look back on than to anticipate, it has returned—not least because of passages like this one. The idea that there is an ultimate reality, a way that things were always intended to be, a spiritual universe that can only be described by reference to itself, is exciting and reassuring. I remember the thrill of seeing real elephants at a zoo when I was a small child. The pictures I had seen in books were just a copy and a shadow of the real thing. Our first sight of the new heaven and earth might be even more exciting than that.

Sunday prayer

Thank you that there is so much more than this.

AP

Ineffably parental

For if there had been nothing wrong with that first covenant, no place would have been sought for another. But God found fault with the people and said: 'The time is coming,' declares the Lord, 'when I will make a new covenant with the house of Israel and with the house of Judah. It will not be like the covenant I made with their forefathers when I took them by the hand to lead them out of Egypt, because they did not remain faithful to my covenant, and I turned away from them,' declares the Lord.

There is something ineffably parental about God, isn't there? Leaving aside the slight differences between the creator of the universe and myself, his ways of dealing with Israel, and indeed with all of his children, remind me so much of the relationship Bridget and I have had with our children over the years. This passage brings to mind those many occasions when we have had to abandon our carefully thought-out plan A because the child it was designed for has failed to agree to his or her part in the arrangement.

Perhaps this makes us angry. Perhaps it makes us turn away, but, as all our fellow parents know, we can only turn away for a season. Why is that? You know why it is. We love them. We love them beyond their disobedience and their refusal to co-operate. Even as the cross expression on our faces is still visible, we are mentally devising a plan B, something that will allow everything to be all right again. A different approach, a new angle, a fresh attempt to produce the right response.

I would suggest that God is doing exactly that here. Being God, he is unable to go against his own nature by turning a blind eye to sin, but neither is the great lover of the world able to turn his back on those he loves with such a passion. In my opinion, our chronic failure to comprehend the ocean of love with which God yearns to flood the Church is responsible for much of the individual spiritual breakdown that is all too common nowadays. God can be very fierce, but watch his eyes…

Prayer

Father, thank you for being so fatherly, so loving. Open our eyes so that we can see you properly.

AP

The golden grace of God

'This is the covenant I will make with the house of Israel after that time, declares the Lord. I will put my laws in their minds and write them on their hearts. I will be their God and they will be my people. No longer will a man teach his neighbour, or a man his brother, saying, "Know the Lord", because they will all know me, from the least of them to the greatest. For I will forgive their wickedness and will remember their sins no more.' By calling this covenant 'new', he has made the first one obsolete; and what is obsolete and ageing will soon disappear.

Well, here is plan B—God's intention of establishing a new (or perhaps very ancient) intimacy between himself and his people, as prophesied by Jeremiah. This plan involved the death and resurrection of Jesus, events that were essential if the Holy Spirit was to come and live in the hearts of men and women as God promises here.

So far, so good—indeed, so far, so exceedingly good. There is one problem, though, and it is one that has made life difficult for many Christians during the last two thousand years. It centres on one of the words in this passage— 'obsolete'. How, my dear brothers and sisters, are we to persuade the sad and striving ones among us that the old covenant really is obsolete and that we are only saved by the golden grace of God?

Yesterday I listened to a troubled young man called Alan who is anxious to follow Jesus, but deeply worried about his acceptability to God. Is he showing the right fruits? Are there enough fruits? Is he being sufficiently sacrificial in his giving of time and money and effort? When he arrives at the gates of heaven, will God look down his nose and refuse to admit this quivering would-be Christian? Alan was and is very tense and concerned.

I told him what I thought. These things are important. Of course we should consider them, but only because, having discovered the freedom that comes from knowing we are loved by God, we now want to please him as much as we can. We are adopted, not employed.

Reflection

Are you motivated by God's love or are you stranded in plan A?

AP

Small world

Now the first covenant had regulations for worship and also an earthly sanctuary. A tabernacle was set up. In its first room were the lampstand, the table and the consecrated bread; this was called the Holy Place. Behind the second curtain was a room called the Most Holy Place, which had the golden altar of incense and the gold-covered ark of the covenant. This ark contained the gold jar of manna, Aaron'.s staff that had budded, and the stone tablets of the covenant. Above the ark were the cherubim of the Glory, overshadowing the atonement cover. But we cannot discuss these things in detail now.

'We cannot discuss these things in detail,' says the writer of Hebrews, having discussed them in considerable detail. I like the detail. I like hearing about the set-up in the tabernacle. I have always been a lover of small worlds. Perhaps that explains why, in the course of my work with children in care, I worked in two different secure units—one in Birmingham and one in Sussex. It was nothing to do with finding enjoyment in locking children up—indeed, whenever possible, the secure unit in Sussex had its doors wide open. No, it was something to do with reducing the big, complicated world to a small, precisely defined area that could be managed with comparative ease and simplicity.

I would love to have gone into the tabernacle, to have moved slowly through the Holy Place and the Most Holy Place, gazing at all those amazing relics and decorations as I went. Imagine poring over the very tablets that Moses had brought down from the mountain or handling the staff that Aaron had once held in his hand.

It is remarkable when we reflect on the fact that the theoretically boundless cosmos of God's communication with man had, for eminently practical reasons, including our inability to handle any but small worlds, been reduced to this tiny area filled with symbols of the greatest escape of all. Even more remarkable is that, in this age, the Holy Spirit is willing to inhabit the small world of your spirit or my spirit, a world where we are allowed to enter the Most Holy Place and meet with the God of the Israelites whenever we wish.

Reflection

I will meet you in the tabernacle of my heart, Lord.

AP

Dad's home!

When everything had been arranged like this, the priests entered regularly into the outer room to carry on their ministry. But only the high priest entered the inner room, and that only once a year, and never without blood, which he offered for himself and for the sins the people had committed in ignorance. The Holy Spirit was showing by this that the way into the Most Holy Place had not yet been disclosed as long as the first tabernacle was still standing. This is an illustration for the present time, indicating that the gifts and sacrifices being offered were not able to clear the conscience of the worshipper. They are only a matter of food and drink and various ceremonial washings—external regulations applying until the time of the new order.

When children are small, they can only manage for a limited time without drawing on the special blend of assurance, affection and natural authority that the best mums and dads are so good at giving them. You can hear children on a thousand street corners, and in ten thousand back gardens, loudly shouting at each other about what they will allow each other to do or not do in the course of a game: 'You have to wait there and I have to come along and you have to not see me until I'm just behind your back and then I have to shoot you...' One of the others replies, 'Yeah, and then I have to come alive again and you have to give me the gun and I have to shoot you...'

The embattled, stentorian tones in which these commands are uttered is some indication of the lack of real confidence that children feel in their self-imposed rules. When mum or dad come back, though, well, it's different. Different ethos. Different sense of safety. Different awareness of love lying at the heart of authority.

God's new order is the same. We are not left on our own any more. He is no longer issuing orders from a distance or sending messages through someone else. Now, we can know for sure that the things we do, good or bad, will be dealt with properly, on the spot, by the only one who really does see right to the heart of what we are. Dad's home.

Prayer
Father, sit on the doorstep and watch us as we play.

AP

A step forward?

When Christ came as high priest of the good things that are already here, he went through the greater and more perfect tabernacle that is not man-made, that is to say, not a part of this creation. He did not enter by means of the blood of goats and calves; but he entered the Most Holy Place once for all by his own blood, having obtained eternal redemption. The blood of goats and bulls and the ashes of a heifer sprinkled on those who are ceremonially unclean sanctify them so that they are outwardly clean. How much more, then, will the blood of Christ, who through the eternal Spirit offered himself unblemished to God, cleanse our consciences from acts that lead to death, so that we may serve the living God!

The exclamation mark at the end of this passage was not my idea. I don't like exclamation marks (other than when they follow exclamations) and I especially loathe them when they are added to the end of a sentence by some self-deluded writer who thinks he has said something clever!

Seriously, though, why is it there? Perhaps it is telling us that something important has just been said. If that is its purpose, I agree with it. I have previously mentioned talking to a young man who was very worried about not being good enough for God. One of his main concerns was that he had never truly been forgiven. He knew the Bible inside out and he quoted it constantly, but it didn't seem to be helping him with his problem. I think if I had produced half a mug of bull's blood, a basin of goat's blood and a pinch of heifer ashes and thrown it over him he might have felt better, but only for a while. Like many others, he is trapped in a little virtual biblical prison. He needs to get out and meet Jesus, who will forgive his past sins once and for all through his own shed blood and be happy to do it again tomorrow when Alan rolls up with a fresh crop of interesting sins to talk about. Perhaps then he will stop worrying about forgiveness and start worrying about how he might serve the living God. That would at least be a step forward!!

Reflection
We really can be clean!!!!

AP

A true picture

For Christ did not enter a man-made sanctuary that was only a copy of the true one; he entered heaven itself, now to appear for us in God's presence. Nor did he enter heaven to offer himself again and again, the way the high priest enters the Most Holy Place every year with blood that is not his own. Then Christ would have had to suffer many times since the creation of the world. But now he has appeared once for all at the end of the ages to do away with sin by the sacrifice of himself. Just as man is destined to die once, and after that to face judgement, so Christ was sacrificed once to take away the sins of many people; and he will appear a second time, not to bear sin, but to bring salvation to those who are waiting for him.

This is a magnificent picture, isn't it? Spielberg would have a job coming up with anything to equal this. I have never been to heaven, but I can dream. After the long history of God's protracted and painful strivings with mankind, Jesus steps into heaven, applauded by the ranks of angels and saints, to claim forgiveness and salvation for Adrian Plass, for you, dear reader, and for one or two others who need not concern us at the moment.

'I've done it!' he exclaims. 'No more tabernacles, no more high priests, no more blood sloshing around. In future, if anyone has anything against Adrian Plass or the person who is reading his Bible notes at this very moment, you can refer them to me. The pain is for ever, but so too is the joy. All debts are paid and death has been overcome. I shall be going back for Adrian and his reader later on.'

A million angels and ten million saints cheer themselves hoarse—in a spiritual sort of way. The devil gnashes his teeth and asks himself where it first went wrong for him.

In case my tone deceives you into thinking I'm joking, I'm not. My life, my future, everything that I am or will ever be depends on the truth of the picture that I have so inadequately painted here. It is reality. You and I will be waiting for him and he will come.

Prayer

Thank you.

AP

Ready to fly?

The law is only a shadow of the good things that are coming—not the realities themselves. For this reason it can never, by the same sacrifices repeated endlessly year after year, make perfect those who draw near to worship. If it could, would they not have stopped being offered? For the worshippers would have been cleansed once for all, and would no longer have felt guilty for their sins. But those sacrifices are an annual reminder of sins, because it is impossible for the blood of bulls and goats to take away sins.

Bridget and I will never forget our first trip to Australia. We had been invited to speak at the first national convention of the Uniting Church, a denomination made up of Methodists, Presbyterians and Congregationalists. We were so excited. Hitherto, our travels had been limited. Imagine flying all that way across the world to a place we had only read about in books and seen on television. It was like a dream.

As the weeks went by, a flood of practical concerns swamped our dream. Katy, our youngest, was coming with us, but that left the three boys, who were 16, 12 and 11. We arranged for friends to move in and look after them while we were away. There were visas to be obtained, one passport to be renewed, clothes to be bought, money to be saved, a week of speaking material to be prepared and a whole host of fears and uncertainties to be faced. In the fortnight before flying, it got so complicated that we lost sight of the reason for our trip. It was difficult to see the object of our efforts amid such a swirling haze of essential but uninspiring considerations.

We left and the dream not only returned, but became a reality that far outstripped our hopes. That first experience of Australia remains in our memories as a truly golden time. We were so warmly welcomed, so well looked after, so much appreciated that, from then onwards and during each of the three trips that we have subsequently made, the country shines like a beacon and will always call us back. All the work and the worry were worth it.

I won't labour the point, but the Law is only a shadow of the golden times that are coming.

Sunday reflection
Ready to fly?

AP

HEBREWS 10:5–10 (NIV)

A simple soul

Therefore, when Christ came into the world, he said: 'Sacrifice and offering you did not desire, but a body you prepared for me; with burnt offerings and sin offerings you were not pleased. Then I said, "Here I am—it is written about me in the scroll—I have come to do your will, O God."' First he said, 'Sacrifices and offerings, burnt offerings and sin offerings you did not desire, nor were you pleased with them' (although the law required them to be made). Then he said, 'Here I am, I have come to do your will.' He sets aside the first to establish the second. And by that will, we have been made holy through the sacrifice of the body of Jesus Christ once for all.

He never has been that interested in the familiar metaphors of sacrifice and worship. Burnt animals, symbolic gifts, ceremonial bun fights and extravaganzas never really touched the spot. They had their place, of course. Filled a gap, as it were. In the purest sense, God has always been a very simple soul. Hope he doesn't mind me saying that. I don't think he will.

No, but it is true. Since the world began, throughout the ages of the Bible, down through the last two thousand years, God has been trying to make his voice heard. 'Look,' says God, 'I don't actually want any of that stuff. It does nothing for me. What I want is for you to be just and kind and to look after the poor. I would like you to be obedient. My son was obedient to the point of death and that's why I'm able to welcome you home. I wouldn't give you tuppence for religion—not even some of the wild, sizzling stuff that's taken the place of burning animals nowadays. Be loving to me and to each other. That's the scent I love—have always loved.'

This is a voice that many people, many Christians, do not want to hear. Too natural, too godly, too liable to insinuate itself into the cracks between our humanity and our faith, supergluing the two together, making us whole, but robbing us of all the old securities. Scary *and* sweet, isn't it?

Prayer

Walk quietly with us in the cool
of the afternoon, Lord.
We need to talk.

AP

The holiness vacuum

Day after day every priest stands and performs his religious duties; again and again he offers the same sacrifices, which can never take away sins. But when this priest had offered for all time one sacrifice for sins, he sat down at the right hand of God. Since that time he waits for his enemies to be made his footstool, because by one sacrifice he has made perfect for ever those who are being made holy. The Holy Spirit also testifies to us about this. First he says: 'This is the covenant I will make with them after that time, says the Lord. I will put my laws in their hearts, and I will write them on their minds.' Then he adds: 'Their sins and lawless acts I will remember no more.' And where these have been forgiven, there is no longer any sacrifice for sin.

There is an intriguing phrase in this passage, one that you have to repeat again and again before it starts making sense: '…by one sacrifice he has made perfect for ever those who are being made holy.' What does this mean? No, it's no good clicking your tongue irritably and saying that you worked it out aeons ago. My brain is the sort that has to take its time.

The people who have been affected by Jesus' sacrifice—people like you and I—have been made perfect by his death on the cross. In other words, we have been turned into qualifiers for heaven, heaven being unable, by its very nature, to admit anything but perfection. Good news. We're in!

In that case, what's this other bit about these same people still being in the process of being made holy, even though they have already been perfected? What does that mean? Well, having considered the question carefully for many minutes, I feel quite encouraged. I know that I am far from holy. I know also that the Holy Spirit has been working slowly on the holiness vacuum in my life for nearly four decades. By the time I reach the grave, I shall still fall far short of perfection, but that, I assume, is when the divine life insurance kicks in—thank God. It may be rubbish theology, but it'll do me.

Reflection
*It's all in hand,
and the hand it's in is pierced.*

AP

HEBREWS 10:19–25 (NIV)

The elbow and the kneecap

Therefore, brothers, since we have confidence to enter the Most Holy Place by the blood of Jesus, by a new and living way opened for us through the curtain, that is, his body, and since we have a great priest over the house of God, let us draw near to God with a sincere heart in full assurance of faith, having our hearts sprinkled to cleanse us from a guilty conscience and having our bodies washed with pure water. Let us hold unswervingly to the hope we profess, for he who promised is faithful. And let us consider how we may spur one another on towards love and good deeds. Let us not give up meeting together, as some are in the habit of doing, but let us encourage one another—and all the more as you see the Day approaching.

Not many people actually draw near to God in full assurance of faith. Lots of Christians, myself included, find that their spiritual confidence dips dramatically at times. Here, in this passage, are four points that might help.

First, are the words 'draw near to God with a sincere heart'. Take the truth of what you are to God, lack of assurance and all. Be straight with him. As we have seen, Jesus died to make up the shortfall. Trust him.

Second, we should spur one another on to good deeds. We take turns at this, being generous with our assurance when we have it and getting plumbed into someone else's when we haven't. We are supposed to be a body.

Meeting together provides the opportunity for such things to happen. I value being alone very highly, but it goes flat in the end—like champagne without a cork. In any case, how long can the body manage without its elbow or its kneecap? Assurance is in the linking of hands, metaphorical or actual.

Encouragement of one another is like the caress of God for a church community. Taking the trouble to recognize value and achievement in our brothers and sisters can have what appears to be a disproportionately positive effect on the recipient. Do you enjoy watching flowers open?

The general message is clear. We're in this together, Jesus and us. Be assured of that and you won't go too far wrong.

Reflection

Jesus had a dark moment on the cross. He understands.

AP

Trampling Elsie

If we deliberately keep on sinning after we have received the knowledge of the truth, no sacrifice for sins is left, but only a fearful expectation of judgment and of raging fire that will consume the enemies of God. Anyone who rejected the law of Moses died without mercy on the testimony of two or three witnesses. How much more severely do you think a man deserves to be punished who has trampled the Son of God under foot, who has treated as an unholy thing the blood of the covenant that sanctified him, and who has insulted the Spirit of grace? For we know him who said, 'It is mine to avenge; I will repay', and again, 'The Lord will judge his people.' It is a dreadful thing to fall into the hands of the living God.

Yes, it is a dreadful thing, but it also isn't. Forgive me, I have a knee-jerk response to this passage. I'll explain.

It was years ago. There were ten people in the Bible study that evening, including one I knew well. Elsie was confident about nothing in her life, including her faith. She was actually a very loyal, generous person, but, as is often the case, she didn't count those qualities as being worth anything at all.

The passage for discussion was the one above. The fellow leading the meeting was the sort of man who speaks softly, but would have no trouble killing rabbits with his bare hands. He read the passage aloud and then spoke with chillingly casual ease about how God will come down on us like a ton of bricks if we put a foot wrong after we've been saved. I looked at my friend. Elsie was fidgeting and looking very troubled. Of course she'd put a foot wrong since becoming a Christian—both feet, several times each. Who hasn't? Elsie obviously feared that she had inadvertently trampled the Son of God underfoot and was now in line for judgement.

For goodness' sake, I thought. We do invite God's fury if we deliberately insult God by ridiculing and diminishing what Jesus has done, but the Elsies of this world have not done that. God loves them and is more than capable of dealing with their heinous crimes.

That's why I reacted to the passage just now as I did.

Prayer
Lord, keep our Elsies safe.

AP

The primal urge

Remember those earlier days after you had received the light, when you stood your ground in a great contest in the face of suffering. Sometimes you were publicly exposed to insult and persecution; at other times you stood side by side with those who were so treated. You sympathised with those in prison and joyfully accepted the confiscation of your property, because you knew that you yourselves had better and lasting possessions.

The picture of anyone joyfully accepting the confiscation of their property is, to my modern Western eyes, almost irresistibly Python-esque: 'Whee! They've taken my stuff! Fantastic! It's all gone! Whee! (Breaks into song) Come on, let's celebrate…!'

It only goes on being funny for a while, though. When my schoolboyish sense of humour has chortled itself to a standstill, I begin to see my own past. Pictures float into my mind of how I used to be, the things I once did, when the staggering awareness of what Jesus had done was still a flashing white light in my consciousness. Oh, I know I was a pain in the neck. I would have avoided myself like the plague. I had a Bible with me constantly and I would talk endlessly to anyone who would listen—and quite a few who wouldn't—about salvation and damnation and the need for them to make a personal commitment immediately because the world might well end before four o'clock that day. It was a passion and a preoccupation. I must have got on so many people's nerves on the streets and in the cafés of Tunbridge Wells.

I was doing it all the same. You know what I mean? I was doing it. I wasn't cuddling my passion for Jesus to myself as I sometimes do nowadays. I was treating the message of salvation as though it was vitally important that others should hear it, letting it flow from me in its raw, shapeless, unrefined state. I probably made a fool of myself from time to time, but that didn't seem to be so much of a problem then.

A lot of what I did was probably bad, but I also suspect that a lot of it was good. The same feeling—that spiritually primal urge—is just beginning to resurface. I'm glad.

Prayer
Catch me, Lord, I'm coming back.

AP

The little ones at the back

So do not throw away your confidence; it will be richly rewarded. You need to persevere so that when you have done the will of God, you will receive what he has promised. For in just a very little while: 'He who is coming will come and will not delay. But my righteous one will live by faith. And if he shrinks back, I will not be pleased with him.' But we are not of those who shrink back and are destroyed, but of those who believe and are saved.

Oh, dear. Am I a back shrinker? Are you?

One of the first stories I told was about my son Matthew, aged , arriving miserably home from school one day. After three tear-dampened jam sandwiches, he explained that, at assembly, the headmistress had frightened him by threatening terrible punishment for any child who brought money to school. Mrs Shaw was frightening—she frightened me. Matthew, shaking in his small shoes, had resolved never to bring a penny to school. Later, in the yard, he put a hand in his pocket and found, to his horror, a coin! Panicking, he tugged it out and dropped it. A passing girl said with relish, 'When I tell Mrs Shaw you brought money to school you'll be in big trouble tomorrow.'

Matthew was terrified. What to do? Simple. I wrote to Mrs Shaw, challenging her to a duel with swords or pistols. If she won she could punish Matthew, if I won she couldn't. A reply arrived the next afternoon.

Mrs Shaw thanked me for making the teachers laugh. It had also made her think carefully about saying loud, forceful things at assembly that were never meant to terrify the little ones at the back. She sounded nice in her letter.

Maybe it was like that with Jesus. After one of his stern pronouncements, a nervous disciple tugs his sleeve and says, 'Look, I don't think I'm up to this!'

'Don't worry,' Jesus replies from the corner of his mouth, 'you're OK. It's that lot over there I'm getting at…'

Don't worry. We'll be as courageous as necessary. We may be the little ones at the back, but we also know that God is almost as nice as Mrs Shaw—perhaps even nicer.

Reflection
Thank goodness she didn't accept my challenge.

AP

Luke's miracles

Is it true? Did it really happen? It's a question that is bound to occur to us when we hear of something unusual happening, something we would have thought impossible. It might be the first thing we ask about the miracles we read in Luke. Certainly many people today would find the Gospels more acceptable if the miracles were not there. It seems to remove them so far from our experience.

Perhaps Luke was facing such questions when he wrote his Gospel. Perhaps there were other stories going round that had little basis in fact. Luke wanted to set the record straight, make sure that his readers knew the truth about Jesus (Luke 1:3–4).

However, for Luke, this is not just the story of a life, it's about the coming of God's kingdom, the beginning of a whole new era. Because of that, asking whether or not the stories are true is only the beginning. We also have to ask what they mean for us. Certainly, Luke wants his readers to know that they are true, but that raises as many questions as it answers.

Over the next two weeks, as we look at some of the miracles in Luke's Gospel, we consider the reactions they provoke and address the questions they raise.

Luke records in Acts that Jesus is 'a man attested to you by God with deeds of power, wonders, and signs' (Acts 2:22, NRSV)—in other words, the miracles show who he is. So, we ask the question, who is Jesus? What do the miracles tell us about him and the God he proclaims? Then we look at the impact the miracles make on the lives of those they touch. This goes far beyond physical healing and has far wider effects than just helping the person who is healed.

We also consider how people responded to the miracles and how we respond today. One big difference between the story of a man who lived two thousand years ago, and who taught some wonderful things about God, and the story of a man who in deed and word claimed to be God, and who rose from the dead, is that this second story, the one Luke presents to us, demands a response. This is why Luke records the miracles and it is something we need to consider as we read them today.

Jane Cornish

89

LUKE 8:23–25 (NRSV)

Who then is this?

While they were sailing he [Jesus] fell asleep. A gale swept down on the lake, and the boat was filling with water, and they were in danger. They went to him and woke him up, shouting, 'Master, Master, we are perishing!' And he woke up and rebuked the wind and the raging waves; they ceased, and there was a calm. He said to them, 'Where is your faith?' They were afraid and amazed, and said to one another, 'Who then is this, that he commands even the winds and the water, and they obey him?'

Who is this? It's not only those who encounter Jesus for the first time who need to ask themselves this question. The disciples have witnessed his miraculous powers before and heard his teaching. They gave up everything to follow him (see 24 July) and, since then, shared the ordinary moments of life with him, got to know his family, ate with him, knew him as a person like themselves.

In today's reading, he is so tired that he falls asleep on the boat and not even the storm wakes him. Once awake, however, he quells the storm with a few words. No wonder the disciples are afraid and amazed—they could not help but realize anew that the person there with them, the man with whom they have become so familiar, is God himself with power over the most uncontrollable forces of nature.

Whether we have been walking with Jesus a long time or a short time, every so often something will happen—in our own life or in what we see around us—that makes us newly amazed at who Jesus is. If we lose that sense of wonder and awe we are in danger of forgetting that he is Emmanuel, God with us, master of creation, yet here 'in the boat' with us.

As we read Luke's account of the miracles that form an integral part of Jesus' life, we need to ask ourselves again, 'Who is this?' Not as if we did not know Jesus, but taking time to let the miracles speak to us about the wonder of God become man, with all that it means for us.

Sunday prayer

Lord, give us a new sense of wonder at who you are.

JC

Are you the one?

When the men had come to him [Jesus], they said, 'John the Baptist has sent us to you to ask, "Are you the one who is to come, or are we to wait for another?"' Jesus had just then cured many people of diseases, plagues, and evil spirits, and had given sight to many who were blind. And he answered them, 'Go and tell John what you have seen and heard: the blind receive their sight, the lame walk, the lepers are cleansed, the deaf hear, the dead are raised, the poor have good news brought to them. And blessed is anyone who takes no offence at me.'

We all have our expectations. At the time of Jesus, God's people lived under Roman rule and looked to the coming of the Messiah to deliver them. John knew he was announcing the coming of someone who would fulfil the prophecies, but things did not work out as he expected. He is in prison and Jesus does not seem to be bringing about the kingdom as John thought he would. So, what was he to think? Look at the miracles, Jesus tells him. The things he is doing are signs that God's kingdom has come—now is the year of the Lord that Isaiah foretold (Luke 4:19; and see Isaiah 61:1–2) and the signs are that people are being released from what held them captive. Jesus is telling John that God's kingdom has come, the prophecy is being fulfilled, but maybe not as he expected.

As we meet with Jesus—whether in the pages of scripture or at work in the world and in our lives today—he often surprises us. Just as he did not act in power to expel the Romans and establish his kingdom on earth, he does not act according to our expectations either. Like John, we might prefer a more spectacular change—God making himself known to the whole world, putting right all the wrong and injustice—but the kingdom of heaven grows quietly in the lives of those who are willing to receive it (Luke 13:18–21). If we can accept his way of working, we shall be blessed by it (7:23).

Reflection

We learn to recognize God's ways as we spend time with him. Take time to get to know him better this week.

JC

None so blind...

As he [Jesus] approached Jericho, a blind man was sitting by the roadside begging. When he heard a crowd going by, he asked what was happening. They told him, 'Jesus of Nazareth is passing by.' Then he shouted, 'Jesus, Son of David, have mercy on me!' Those who were in front sternly ordered him to be quiet; but he shouted even more loudly, 'Son of David, have mercy on me!' Jesus stood still and ordered the man to be brought to him; and when he came near, he asked him, 'What do you want me to do for you?' He said, 'Lord, let me see again.' Jesus said to him, 'Receive your sight; your faith has saved you.' Immediately he regained his sight and followed him, glorifying God; and all the people, when they saw it, praised God.

Here is a man who has not only never seen a miracle, he has never set eyes on Jesus. However, his blindness is not a handicap when it comes to recognizing the important things!

First, he sees Jesus. Physically, of course, he does not, and has to ask who it is that is coming. Then he recognizes that this Jesus of Nazareth is the Son of David, the promised Messiah. Here is someone who can help him. He also sees his need. Jesus' question may seem strange (v. 41), but every gift brings responsibility. He brings wholeness and turns us from our helplessness and dependency to taking responsibility for ourselves. It is wonderful, but it can also be scary.

Finally, the man sees the way ahead. No longer does he have to sit by the road as life goes by; he is free to go his own way. The way he chooses is the way of Jesus.

Jesus asks each one of us, 'What do you want me to do for you?' When life is going well, it is easy to delude ourselves that we do not need anything and we can forget our dependence on God. This is the worst kind of blindness (Revelation 3:17) for only as we come to God for his healing touch can he give us what we need to live for him and follow him day by day.

Prayer

Lord, open my eyes to what you want to do in my life today.

JC

LUKE 11:14–18a, 20, 23 (NRSV)

...as those who will not see

Now he [Jesus] was casting out a demon that was mute; when the demon had gone out, the one who had been mute spoke, and the crowds were amazed. But some of them said, 'He casts out demons by Beelzebul, the ruler of the demons.' Others, to test him, kept demanding from him a sign from heaven. But he knew what they were thinking and said to them, 'Every kingdom divided against itself becomes a desert, and house falls on house. If Satan also is divided against himself, how will his kingdom stand?... But if it is by the finger of God that I cast out the demons, then the kingdom of God has come to you... Whoever is not with me is against me, and whoever does not gather with me scatters.'

The blind man didn't need sight to realize who Jesus was, but others don't believe the evidence of their eyes. What makes them so blind to the truth? One factor is that they have made up their minds. God is constantly doing new things and not to recognize this is to miss his blessing. Jesus the Messiah did not fulfil everybody's expectations and God is too great to be squeezed into our small conceptions of him.

There was another reason for those in today's reading not understanding. To acknowledge Jesus would mean responding to who he is. Those who did not want to be changed or challenged were forced to come up with another explanation, one that did not require them to act (v. 15).

The kingdom of God is a reality for those who can accept it. If we cannot see God in the lives of those who follow him, the world he has created and the teachings of the Bible, a miracle may not help very much, for we shall find a way of explaining that away, too (Luke 16:29–31).

When we do catch a glimpse of God at work, a response is required. He presents us with a challenge: are you for me or against me? Are you willing to be drawn in, to accept God's kingdom with all its implications for your life? To refuse to respond to his claims is to deny their importance (Luke 11:31–32).

Reflection

*How can I be a gatherer,
not a scatterer?*

JC

A deeper need

Just then some men came, carrying a paralysed man on a bed... finding no way to bring him in because of the crowd, they went up on the roof and let him down with his bed... into the middle of the crowd in front of Jesus. When he saw their faith, he said, 'Friend, your sins are forgiven you.' Then the scribes and the Pharisees began to question, 'Who is this who is speaking blasphemies? Who can forgive sins but God alone?'... he [Jesus] answered them, '...Which is easier, to say, "Your sins are forgiven you" or to say, "Stand up and walk"? But so that you may know that the Son of Man has authority on earth to forgive sins'—he said to the one who was paralyzed—'I say to you, stand up and take your bed and go to your home.' Immediately he stood up before them, took what he had been lying on, and went to his home, glorifying God.

What first made you seek out Jesus? This man had a clear need; he was paralysed and he wanted healing. His friends helped him, resorting to desperate measures to get near Jesus. When they do, Jesus does not do what they expect. They thought they knew what was needed, but Jesus saw deeper. They sought physical healing, but Jesus offers new life. He restores the paralysed man to health, but he also restores his relationship with God. Guilt, too, can be paralysing and hearing our forgiveness spoken is a powerfully releasing force.

Of course, forgiveness has to be real. Only because of who Jesus is does he have the authority to announce God's forgiveness. The physical healing of the man is a sign of his inward healing, for God has given Jesus the power to bring both.

When we bring our friends to Jesus we may be surprised at what he does in their lives, and in our own as well. One thing is certain, however—here is a man with authority to speak for God, get to the heart of our need and meet it in more profound ways than we could ever have imagined.

Prayer

Thank you, Lord, that you know my needs and that you are the one who can meet them all.

JC

Not just one of the crowd

Now there was a woman who had been suffering from haemorrhages for twelve years; and though she had spent all she had on physicians, no one could cure her. She came up behind him [Jesus] and touched the fringe of his clothes, and immediately her haemorrhage stopped. Then Jesus asked, 'Who touched me?' When all denied it, Peter said, 'Master, the crowds surround you and press in on you.' But Jesus said, 'Someone touched me; for I noticed that power had gone out from me.' When the woman saw that she could not remain hidden, she came trembling; and falling down before him, she declared in the presence of all the people why she had touched him, and how she had been immediately healed. He said to her, 'Daughter, your faith has made you well; go in peace.'

One of the signs of God's kingdom is release (4:18). Here was a woman whose illness held her captive—to suffering, poverty and exclusion from society (Leviticus 15:25–30). Jesus gave her status as well as health.

There was one more thing that she needed, however. Just as the paralysed man in yesterday's reading needed to know that he was forgiven, this woman needed to know that she was loved. Her healing was not just a matter of magic, an overflowing of power snatched from an unknowing stranger, but the willingly given gift of a loving God. Jesus cares enough about this outcast from society to stop on his way to see the sick child of a synagogue leader and find out who she is. He calls her 'daughter' and speaks to her of wholeness and peace; from being poor, unwell and marginalized, she has become well, accepted and valued.

We may come to Jesus to get our needs met, but, until we have the relationship with God that he intended, our life is incomplete. Jesus offers us that wholeness. Like the woman, we might be tempted to take what God has to give and then fade back into the crowd. Jesus' challenge is that we come forward to meet him and tell others all that he has done for us. Unless we do, we may be missing out on the blessings he longs to give us.

Reflection
To God you are not just one of a crowd, but an individual whom he understands and loves.

JC

From now on...

When he [Jesus] had finished speaking, he said to Simon, 'Put out into the deep water and let down your nets for a catch.' Simon answered, 'Master, we have worked all night long but have caught nothing. Yet if you say so, I will let down the nets.' When they had done this, they caught so many fish that their nets were beginning to break... But when Simon Peter saw it, he fell down at Jesus' knees, saying, 'Go away from me, Lord, for I am a sinful man!' For he and all who were with him were amazed at the catch of fish... Then Jesus said to Simon, 'Do not be afraid; from now on you will be catching people.' When they had brought their boats to shore, they left everything and followed him.

Sometimes when we tell people about Jesus, we come up against a wall of disbelief. More often, they are just not concerned. Their reaction, in attitude if not words, is, 'What's it got to do with me?' The crowds who saw the miracles were a bit like that. They were amazed by what Jesus did, but it didn't change their lives. Before their call, Simon and the other disciples came into the same category.

Suddenly, Jesus is not just asking for a boat to help with his ministry, but telling them how to do their work! Simon, unsure how to react at first, does what Jesus says and the result is that, suddenly, Jesus and his miracles make a difference in their every-day world. Jesus calls them to respond not with fear, but by following him.

Whatever our day-to-day life is like, Jesus wants to be involved in the whole of it. We should expect to meet him there, hear his call and see him at work in everything we do. He does not want us to be afraid, either of what the future might bring or what he might ask of us, but trust him with our whole life and involve him in every detail of it. Following, not fear, is what he wants.

Reflection

The disciples had been up all night fishing without catching anything. Do we sometimes waste our effort by not listening to what Jesus tells us to do?

JC

LUKE 1:30–38 (NRSV, ABRIDGED)

The servant of the Lord

The angel said to her [Mary], 'Do not be afraid, Mary, for you have found favour with God. And now, you will conceive in your womb and bear a son, and you will name him Jesus. He will be great, and will be called the Son of the Most High...' Mary said to the angel, 'How can this be, since I am a virgin?' The angel said to her, 'The Holy Spirit will come upon you, and the power of the Most High will overshadow you; therefore the child to be born will be holy; he will be called Son of God... For nothing will be impossible with God.' Then Mary said, 'Here am I, the servant of the Lord; let it be with me according to your word.'

In many of the miracles, we see Jesus responding to human need, but this, the first miracle Luke records (like the last one in the Gospel), is something different entirely. Here is God breaking through the natural order, working with his power to establish his kingdom.

Like the other miracles, though, this one demands a response. Mary, like Zechariah before her (Luke 1:8–20), wonders how such a thing can happen, but, unlike him, she does not demand proof and accepts the angel's explanation. She responds with faith and obedience, accepting the miracle with all its implications for her life.

If I had been in Mary's position, I feel that there are a lot more questions I would like to have asked. Fore example, 'How am I supposed to explain this to Joseph?' and 'How will I deal with this special child?' No doubt these and many more questions did go through her mind, but she is willing to trust God for the future and accept his plans for her.

The God who works miracles also calls us into his service to participate and work with him. We are not given all the answers and serving the God for whom nothing is impossible (v. 37) does not mean that life will run smoothly or the way that we want it to. Our response to God's greatness and his call can only be one of obedience, entrusting the future to him and serving him when we see miracles and when we do not.

Sunday prayer

Lord, help us to respond to your call with faith and obedience.

JC

Filled with fury

On another sabbath he [Jesus] entered the synagogue and taught, and there was a man there whose right hand was withered. The scribes and the Pharisees watched him to see whether he would cure on the sabbath, so that they might find an accusation against him. Even though he knew what they were thinking, he said to the man who had the withered hand, 'Come and stand here.' He got up and stood there. Then Jesus said to them, 'I ask you, is it lawful to do good or to do harm on the sabbath, to save life or to destroy it?' After looking around at all of them, he said to him, 'Stretch out your hand.' He did so, and his hand was restored. But they were filled with fury and discussed with one another what they might do to Jesus.

Not everybody was delighted with Jesus' miracles. Some people failed to ask the seemingly obvious questions—'Who is it that can do this?' 'What does this mean for me?'—and instead asked, 'Does this fit with the rules?' The restoration of the man's hand brought the Pharisees no joy. They focused instead on the rules Jesus seemed to be breaking, and took offence.

The trouble is that we can all behave like the scribes and Pharisees. It is easier to carry on the way we always have than to be open to new ways of working that seem at odds with what we have always cherished. Of course, there are times when we can't compromise (probably far fewer than we think!), but we need to distinguish between eternal truths and cultural customs that may hinder others from coming to Christ and finding healing and wholeness.

Jesus' work in our life is not always comfortable. He comes to challenge our ways of thinking, to change and deepen our perception of God. He sets us at odds with those who should be our allies as he tells us to 'stand here' (v. 8) and be counted as one whom he heals, at the cost of anything that separates us from the God who then and now is at work in our midst in all sorts of unexpected ways.

Prayer

Lord, give me grace to be open to the new ways you want to work in my life.

JC

Where are the other nine?

As he [Jesus] entered a village, ten lepers approached him. Keeping their distance, they called out, saying, 'Jesus, Master, have mercy on us!' When he saw them, he said to them, 'Go and show yourselves to the priests.' And as they went, they were made clean. Then one of them, when he saw that he was healed, turned back, praising God with a loud voice. He prostrated himself at Jesus' feet and thanked him. And he was a Samaritan. Then Jesus asked, 'Were not ten made clean? But the other nine, where are they? Was none of them found to return and give praise to God except this foreigner?' Then he said to him, 'Get up and go on your way; your faith has made you well.'

What were the lepers' thoughts as Jesus sent them away? Did they expect to be healed (for there was no other reason to show themselves to the priests) or did they think Jesus would do nothing? When they were healed, only one went back to thank him.

'Your faith has made you well', Jesus tells him. Of course all ten lepers had been healed, but the one who came back was truly made whole. Responding in gratitude to Jesus meant that he had been saved from the preoccupation with himself and his own need that makes it impossible for God to work in our lives.

Gratitude is good for our spiritual health. As we look outwards from ourselves to God and others, we become truly free, truly whole. This is the challenge that Luke's Gospel presents: how do we respond to the Jesus of the miracles? Will he see us again or shall we take what we feel we need and go our way? Our healing is in our own hands.

The healed leper was a Samaritan, Luke tells us. When we are established members of God's family, we can begin, without noticing it, to take his blessings for granted. When we see prayers answered, do we take time to go back to God in thanks and praise? It should not need the example of a newcomer to remind us to continue to respond in gratitude and service for all that God has done for us.

Reflection
Read John 6:26–27. What do you want from Jesus?

JC

Amazing transformation, extraordinary God

Then they [Jesus and his disciples] arrived at the country of the Gerasenes... a man of the city who had demons met him... Jesus... commanded the unclean spirit to come out of the man... the demons came out of the man and entered the swine, and the herd rushed down the steep bank into the lake and was drowned... Then all the people of the surrounding country of the Gerasenes asked Jesus to leave them; for they were seized with great fear. So he got into the boat and returned. The man from whom the demons had gone begged that he might be with him; but Jesus sent him away, saying, 'Return to your home, and declare how much God has done for you.'

Asked in a survey if she believed in a God who intervened in everyday life, one woman replied, 'No, just the ordinary kind'. Such a God is not only easier to believe in, in our materialistic age, he is also far less demanding, because if he does not act, we do not need to respond. However, here, once again, we see Jesus acting with transforming power as evil is overcome, a man is healed and an outcast is restored to society.

This man's life is turned round in a most dramatic way (for the full story of how Jesus healed this demon-possessed man, read Luke 8:26–39) and he wants to be with Jesus. Jesus, though, gives him a different challenge: go home and tell others what God has done. This will not be easy among these people who are not sure that they want this uncomfortable, uncontrollable God in their lives. They sent Jesus away (v. 37) and may not want to hear anything good that anyone has to say about him. They cannot fail to see the transformation in this man's life, however, and this gives him a strong point from which to begin.

How do we speak to others about our life-transforming God when it is so much easier to believe in the 'ordinary kind'? Telling people about the difference Jesus makes to us can help them see beyond the remote, unknown God to the Saviour who is involved, who heals and makes us anew.

Reflection
When Jesus is asked to leave, he does. Only those who want him to stay and be involved will see their lives transformed.

JC

You give them something to eat

The day was drawing to a close, and the twelve came to him [Jesus] and said, 'Send the crowd away, so that they may go into the surrounding villages and countryside, to lodge and get provisions; for we are here in a deserted place.' But he said to them, 'You give them something to eat.' They said, 'We have no more than five loaves and two fish—unless we are to go and buy food for all these people.' For there were about five thousand men. And he said to his disciples, 'Make them sit down in groups of about fifty each.' They did so and made them all sit down. And taking the five loaves and the two fish, he looked up to heaven, and blessed and broke them, and gave them to the disciples to set before the crowd. And all ate and were filled.

The disciples are overwhelmed with the situation. They are faced with crowds of hungry people at the end of the day—what were they supposed to do? They want Jesus to take charge, but he turns the situation back on them—'You give them something to eat.'

If they had just decided to share their food around, they would not have had anything like enough to feed such a large crowd. Because Jesus called them to act with him and gave his blessing, they found that they had far more than they needed (v. 17), for more than 5000 people.

Sometimes what we want is for God to make everything right, but Jesus tells us, 'You do it'. If we let ourselves feel overwhelmed by the size of the task and the limitations of our resources, the situation remains hopeless. If we hoard what we have, afraid to offer it to Jesus, either because we want it ourselves or fear that it is not good enough for him, the crowd will remain unfed.

When we go to Jesus knowing that we are at the end of our resources, he can take what we offer him and it is more than enough.

Reflection

Read how Peter and John act with Jesus' power, giving what they have (Acts 3:1–10). Sometimes we think we need God to give us something different when he wants us simply to use what we have.

JC

The really important thing

The seventy returned with joy, saying, 'Lord, in your name even the demons submit to us!' He said to them, 'I watched Satan fall from heaven like a flash of lightning. See, I have given you authority to tread on snakes and scorpions, and over all the power of the enemy; and nothing will hurt you. Nevertheless, do not rejoice at this, that the spirits submit to you, but rejoice that your names are written in heaven.'

What is the most important thing about the miracles? We have seen people whose lives were transformed as Jesus made them well, but it was those who responded to him in gratitude and worship who were really made whole (Luke 8:47; 17:16). It is as Jesus plays a lasting part in our lives that the miracles become truly meaningful. The disciples in our reading here are thrilled at the power Jesus has given them, but Jesus points them back to their relationship with him.

Reading about the miracles that Jesus and the early Church performed, perhaps hearing of spectacular things happening in some churches today, we may wonder if something is missing from our Christian experience, but the important thing, Jesus reminds us, is that we are close to him. Some have amazing gifts, a few are called to spectacular ministries, but if we are walking with Jesus and know that he has saved us, then we are whole—our life is given meaning by our relationship with him. Sir James Young Simpson, who pioneered the use of chloroform, was once asked what his greatest discovery was. He answered, 'My greatest discovery was that Jesus Christ is my Saviour.'

The disciples are diverted by the spectacular. Perhaps the danger for us is not so much this—it is hardly a regular occurrence for most of us—but that, having grown used to being Christians, we will cease to be amazed by what Jesus has done for us. What could be greater than the miracle of new birth and transformation he has performed and is reliving in us daily? Whatever else happens or does not happen, our relationship with him continues to be the most important thing of all.

Reflection
What do you really value? Take time to think of all that Jesus has done for you—and rejoice!

JC

A new dawn

But on the first day of the week, at early dawn, they [the women] came to the tomb, taking the spices that they had prepared. They found the stone rolled away from the tomb, but when they went in, they did not find the body. While they were perplexed about this, suddenly two men in dazzling clothes stood beside them. The women were terrified and bowed their faces to the ground, but the men said to them, 'Why do you look for the living among the dead? He is not here, but has risen.'

Our reading takes place at the beginning of a new day, a new week, but for the disciples it is all over. The one who saved others apparently could not save himself (23:35) and their hopes are at an end. If Jesus is dead, what had the last three years been all about? Into their despair this greatest of miracles breaks like the dawn, transforming their despair and terror into new life and new hope. It is not the end of the story but a glorious beginning, and the disciples are called to be witnesses (24:48).

It does not happen all at once. First, the women find the empty tomb. Then, gradually more and more disciples see Jesus and hear his call. Even as Jesus returns to heaven, in many ways they have not really understood (Acts 1:6). However, they are the ones Jesus has chosen to work through and with so he helps them understand the scriptures (Luke 24:45) and sends his Holy Spirit to empower them (Acts 1:8).

We started off by asking why Luke recorded the miracles that Jesus did. Like the first disciples, he felt called to bear witness to what he knew and had experienced of Jesus. We were not there either, but, like Luke, we have heard the message of how Jesus can transform our lives and, like him and those Jesus healed, whose lives he turned round, we are called to be witnesses to him. He will equip us as he equipped the first disciples and, with his help, the task is not too great!

Reflection

At the end of these notes, ask yourself, 'Who is Jesus? What impact have the miracle stories had on me? How will I respond?'

JC

Bible places

Places are important to us—our place of birth, home town, sites we have visited on holiday or pilgrimage, burial places of relatives and friends. Things happen in places—words are spoken, changes occur, friendships are made or broken. There are probably places for each of us that we shall never forget, for one reason or another.

Places are also important in God's story or, at any rate, the story of his dealings with the human race. Just think of some of them—Eden, Ararat, Ur of the Chaldees, Sinai, Canaan, Jordan, Bethlehem, Jerusalem. It would be no exaggeration to say that the history of our faith is largely the history of people... and places.

In the next fortnight, we shall be looking at some of the places in the Bible, especially those that in this holiday season might be places of pilgrimage or we may encounter as names of places of worship (especially in Wales, I have to say!) Some of these place-names also figure prominently in the older hymns—Zion, Jordan, Carmel, Bethel and so on.

One of the values of identifying Bible places is that it reminds us that our religion is based on geography and history. The Hebrew scriptures (Old Testament) tell the story of God's dealings with a particular people in a particular setting and their growing understanding of his nature, power and love. The New Testament takes place in very specific locations—Galilee, Jerusalem, Damascus, Antioch, Philippi and the rest. These narratives are not like Aesop's Fables, stories with a moral but unrelated to actual people and events. Just look at the prologue to Luke's Gospel to see how important it was for him that these things had really happened to real people.

So, as we travel back in time to the days of the patriarchs, to Bethel, Sinai and Peniel or, in the time of Jesus, to Siloam, Bethlehem or Bethesda, the places of the Bible will help remind us that our God is a God who comes to people in the places where they are. Eventually, of course, this commitment to place became sublime in the incarnate Son of God, who lived among us (John 1:14) and, by his presence, made many simple local names immortal. What would Galilee be today if Jesus had not walked its shores?

David Winter

Jerusalem, the Golden

I was glad when they said to me, 'Let us go to the house of the Lord!' Our feet are standing within your gates, O Jerusalem. Jerusalem—built as a city that is bound firmly together. To it the tribes go up, the tribes of the Lord, as was decreed for Israel, to give thanks to the name of the Lord... Pray for the peace of Jerusalem: 'May they prosper who love you. Peace be within your walls, and security within your towers.'

It's hard to distinguish between the real Jerusalem—the geographical location of the city of this name that has stood on more or less the same site for over 3000 years—and the almost mystical idea of Jerusalem that runs all through the Bible. It has had several names, including Salem (much loved as a chapel name!), Zion (same again), the city of David and Jerusalem—all of them full of religious significance. Perhaps because of its position—a city set on hills and dominating the surrounding landscape—it has been a strategic site since ancient times.

Eventually, David drove the Jebusites out of it (2 Samuel 5:6–9) and established it as the 'capital' city of Israel. There, during the reign of his son Solomon, the first great temple of the Lord was built. It became the centre of the nation's worship, the only place where sacrifices could be made to the Lord and a required place of pilgrimage. This psalm is known as one of the 'Songs of Ascent', so called because its words were to be sung as worshippers made their way up the slopes towards the temple, finally ascending a long and grand stairway.

It captures two wonderful spiritual experiences. The first is the joy of the worship of the Lord—'I was glad...' There might be a word there to rebuke us when we wake on a Sunday morning and feel that the last thing we want to do is go to church. The second is the invocation of peace—as relevant now as ever. Peace in Jerusalem, certainly, is a current as well as a historical concern—it has been a hotbed of strife for centuries—but also peace within the 'new Jerusalem', the people of the kingdom of heaven.

Sunday reflection

To pray for peace and to pray for unity ('bound firmly together') is really one prayer, isn't it?

DW

Bethel, the house of God

He [Jacob] came to a certain place and stayed there for the night, because the sun had set. Taking one of the stones of the place, he put it under his head and lay down... And he dreamed that there was a ladder set up on the earth, the top of it reaching to heaven; and the angels of God were ascending and descending on it. And the Lord stood beside him and said, 'I am the Lord, the God of Abraham your father and the God of Isaac; the land on which you lie I will give to you and to your offspring... I will not leave you until I have done what I have promised you.' Then Jacob woke from his sleep and said, 'Surely the Lord is in this place—and I did not know it!'... and he took the stone that he had put under his head and set it up for a pillar and poured oil on the top of it. He called that place Bethel.

Hebrew scholars may dispute it, but it certainly sounds as though Bethel means 'house of God'. Certainly that was how Jacob saw this awesome place. Resting there on his first night after running away from home to avoid what he assumed would be Esau's fury at being cheated out of his birthright, he used a rock for a pillow and dreamt (quite an achievement, I reckon!). In his dream or vision he saw a ladder from earth to heaven, with angels ascending and descending on it.

It is the ultimate spiritual vision, surely—a means of access to God and a way of receiving from God, just as a ladder can connect us to the loft of a house. Jesus used this very image when he spoke to Nathaniel (John 1:51), for he is the perfect 'ladder' between Earth and heaven, between the eternal God and his earthly people.

It is worth reading this story in full because it is, in a sense, the account of Jacob's conversion. More than that, it is literally awe-inspiring—Yahweh, the Lord, touching the runaway in a manner that convinces him that he has been visited by God.

Reflection

No wonder he called the place 'Bethel', which means 'Surely the Lord is in this place'. We need to cherish our 'Bethels', the priceless places of meeting with him.

DW

Peniel, the face of God

Jacob was left alone; and a man wrestled with him until daybreak. When the man saw that he did not prevail against Jacob, he struck him on the hip socket; and Jacob's hip was put out of joint as he wrestled with him. Then he said, 'Let me go, for the day is breaking.' But Jacob said, 'I will not let you go, unless you bless me.' So he said to him, 'What is your name?' And he said, 'Jacob.' Then the man said, 'You shall no longer be called Jacob, but Israel, for you have striven with God and with humans, and have prevailed.' Then Jacob asked him, 'Please tell me your name.' But he said, 'Why is it that you ask my name?' And there he blessed him. So Jacob called the place Peniel, saying, 'For I have seen God face to face, and yet my life is preserved.' The sun rose upon him as he passed Penuel, limping because of his hip.

A second strange and mystical encounter of Jacob's gives us another name for those huge, remote Welsh chapels—Peniel (or Penuel), which means 'the face of God'. The context of the story is important. Jacob had decided that the time had come to seek reconciliation with his wronged brother Esau and is on the way to meet him, conveying various gifts in the form of sheep and cattle as peace offerings. Perhaps his sleep was troubled at the thought of the encounter that lay ahead. He had certainly wrestled with his conscience about it. Now, in a night vision, he wrestled with a mysterious and unnamed challenger, the fight being prolonged. Jacob was not going to submit, even though the secret wrestler had disabled his thigh, but he was not prepared to let the man go 'until he blessed him'. This suggests that Jacob recognized some divine element in the encounter. Later Jewish tradition identified the opponent as an angel of the Lord, though, in fact, he refused to identify himself.

However, he did bless Jacob, though the night's experience left him crippled. Apparently refreshed by this encounter, the erstwhile cheat set off the next morning to meet his brother, limping into the sunrise.

Reflection

Sometimes our most profound spiritual experiences leave us with a painful mark, but also enable us to face the challenges of the new day.

DW

Sinai, the place of the Law

When all the people witnessed the thunder and lightning, the sound of the trumpet, and the mountain smoking, they were afraid and trembled and stood at a distance, and said to Moses, 'You speak to us, and we will listen; but do not let God speak to us, or we will die.' Moses said to the people, 'Do not be afraid; for God has come only to test you and to put the fear of him upon you so that you do not sin.' Then the people stood at a distance, while Moses drew near to the thick darkness where God was.

The Israelites must have felt that they had seen it all when God parted the waters for them to escape from Egypt. Then there was the gift of manna to feed them and water from the rock. By day they could see the pillar of cloud ahead and by night they rested under the protection of the pillar of fire. Yet, nothing had prepared them for Sinai, where they now camped on Moses' instructions.

Clearly something of great significance was about to happen. The mountain began to smoke, like an extinct volcano bursting into life. There were rumblings and cracks of thunder, lightning so terrible that the mountain shook. In the midst of the turmoil, Moses made his way up the mountain. What did it all mean?

This was the second defining moment in their history. God's people were to receive the divine Law by which their personal lives, society and religion would be shaped for ever. The display of God's power was to remind them that this was not the passing on of ethical principles to be debated, but of divine law to be obeyed. It was for their good, but the Law—set out in the Ten Commandments, but expanded into a detailed pattern of behaviour for this newly created nation—needed to be received with 'fear' (reverence) if it was to keep them from sin.

Reflection

We misunderstand the role of the Law in Judaism if we think of it simply as a yoke that they were unable to bear (Acts 15:10). That was how it had become as a result of the interpretations and additions of the scribes, but the Law of the Lord is a source of joy to those who live by it (see Psalm 119:1–3, 14–16).

DW

Jericho—the unlikely victory

Then Joshua rose early in the morning, and the priests took up the ark of the Lord. The seven priests carrying the seven trumpets of rams' horns before the ark of the Lord passed on, blowing the trumpets continually. The armed men went before them, and the rearguard came after the ark of the Lord, while the trumpets blew continually. On the second day they marched around the city once and then returned to the camp. They did this for six days. On the seventh day they rose early, at dawn, and marched around the city in the same manner seven times. It was only on that day that they marched around the city seven times. And at the seventh time, when the priests had blown the trumpets, Joshua said to the people, 'Shout! For the Lord has given you the city.'

'And the walls came tumbling down!' Everyone knows the story of how 'Joshua fit the battle of Jericho', but in reality it was no laughing matter—certainly not for the inhabitants, who were ruthlessly put to the sword by Joshua's army (v. 21). Whatever way we look at it, the fall of Jericho was a triumph for the Israelite people, fresh from crossing the Jordan and entering the promised land, but a disaster for everyone else. Of course, if they were to possess the land God had promised them, Jericho had to be overcome, because it stood like an ancient sentinel over the route to the fertile lands to the east.

For the narrator, however, and for us as we read the story in the passage today, those were not the prime issues. For him, it was a glorious victory for the Lord, a vindication of his promises to his people. Yet again, as when the Israelites finally left Egypt, it was achieved without any effort on the part of the people—they stood back and saw the salvation of their God. Their contribution to the fall of this apparently impregnable walled city was simply to obey his commands. The obedience was theirs; the victory was his.

Reflection

Most of us face 'impregnable walled cities' from time to time. There are situations that seem to be beyond us, opposition that seems impenetrable, problems with which we can't cope. Instead of bashing our heads against them, should we try some simple trust?

DW

Ebenezer—stone of help

The people of Israel said to Samuel, 'Do not cease to cry out to the Lord our God for us, and pray that he may save us from the hand of the Philistines.' So Samuel took a sucking lamb and offered it as a whole burnt offering to the Lord; Samuel cried out to the Lord for Israel, and the Lord answered him. As Samuel was offering up the burnt offering, the Philistines drew near to attack Israel; but the Lord thundered with a mighty voice that day against the Philistines and threw them into confusion; and they were routed before Israel... Then Samuel took a stone and set it up between Mizpah and Jeshanah, and named it Ebenezer; for he said, 'Thus far the Lord has helped us.' So the Philistines were subdued and did not again enter the territory of Israel...

You can see them in many a Welsh valley—vast chapels dominating the landscape, capable of seating, one imagines, the entire population and once, in times of revival, doubtless full of people raising the roof with their hymns. Then there's the name, carved in stone above the imposing doorway: 'Ebenezer: hitherto hath the Lord helped us'.

It all goes back to this story from the days of the Judges of Israel, to the time of the last great prophet-judge Samuel. The Philistines had been a sore trial to the people as they sought to settle in the promised land, but now, in what at the time looked like a decisive battle, the Lord himself intervened with a voice of thunder and the menacing ranks fled before the soldiers of Israel. The Philistines 'did not again enter the territory of Israel', the narrator optimistically claimed. In fact, not many years later, the young David, himself anointed by Samuel, would be facing them, led by their giant warrior Goliath.

That very fact emphasizes the message of the name 'Ebenezer', for its proper translation is not 'hitherto', but 'thus far'. All of God's help is 'thus far' or, as we might put it, 'day by day'. You can't store it away for future use, but, at the time of need, it is always to hand.

Reflection

To this point, to this day of our lives, God has been our helper. That's the evidence that he will also stand by us in the future.

DW

Hermon—the mount of blessing

How very good and pleasant it is when kindred live together in unity! It is like the precious oil on the head, running down upon the beard, on the beard of Aaron, running down over the collar of his robes. It is like the dew of Hermon, which falls on the mountains of Zion. For there the Lord ordained his blessing, life for evermore.

Hermon is by far the highest mountain in the whole region of Palestine and its triple peaks dominated the ancient land of Israel. They stand over 9000 feet above sea level and are snow-capped all year. Thus it was that Hermon provided a ready source of water, both for the Jordan river and also to water the lands of northern Israel. The melting waters overflowed from pools near the summit and ran down the sides of the mountain, providing the psalmist with the memorable picture of Aaron's beard dripping with the oil of priestly anointing.

In popular thought, this is the mountain of the transfiguration (Mark 9:2–8), but its height makes this unlikely. It remains, however, a lofty symbol of the constant running water of God's blessing, which, in this short but lovely psalm, is seen as the blessing of unity. From the heights of heaven, as it were, the blessing of God flows down on those who 'live together in unity'.

Unity is one of those things that Christians talk about a lot, but find rather more difficult in practice! Sometimes it is easier to relegate issues of unity to matters far removed from the detail of our home and local church lives, to make it all a question of churches and denominations coming together. However, the whole thrust of this psalm is that those who are 'kindred' should live in unity, which seems to make it much more an issue for my family and my local congregation than for the denomination or wider grouping to which I belong. God wants us to 'live together in unity', visibly and practically—something for which Jesus prayed (John 17:21)—and when we do, the streams of Hermon will bring his blessing.

Reflection

Just as the waters of Hermon bring life to dry and parched ground, so the blessings of unity bring 'life for evermore'.

DW

Carmel—the mount of decision

[Elijah said to Ahab] 'Now therefore have all Israel assemble for me at Mount Carmel, with the 450 prophets of Baal and the 400 prophets of Asherah, who eat at Jezebel's table.' So Ahab... assembled the prophets at Mount Carmel. Elijah then came near to all the people, and said, 'How long will you go limping with two different opinions? If the Lord is God, follow him; but if Baal, then follow him.' The people did not answer him a word. Then Elijah said to the people, 'I, even I only, am left a prophet of the Lord; but Baal's prophets number 450. Let two bulls be given to us; let them choose one bull for themselves, cut it in pieces, and lay it on the wood, but put no fire to it; I will prepare the other bull and lay it on the wood, but put no fire to it. Then you call on the name of your god and I will call on the name of the Lord; the god who answers by fire is indeed God.' All the people answered, 'Well spoken!'

This is part of the long story of Elijah's confrontation with the prophets of Baal, who had been encouraged by the queen, Jezebel, and whose practices had been widely accepted by the people of Israel. The prophet decides that this evil must be confronted and summons both the people (presumably, a representative crowd) and the prophets of Baal themselves to gather on Carmel for this decisive showdown.

Carmel—the name means 'fruitful garden'—is a hill near the coast and to the north-west of Jerusalem. Here, Elijah proposes this 'test by fire'. Needless to say, despite hours of imploring, no fire fell in response to the prayers of the prophets of Baal. Elijah then doused the other bull in water three times. When he called on the Lord, fire fell from heaven and consumed the sacrifice. The people chanted, 'The Lord is indeed God', and Elijah was vindicated (vv. 25–40).

Sunday reflection

Elijah wrongly thought that only he was left faithful to the Lord— a common enough delusion! As we worship today with fellow Christians all around the world, may our offering, too, confirm our faith and glorify our God.

DW

Galilee—the place of good news

Now after John was arrested, Jesus came to Galilee, proclaiming the good news of God, and saying, 'The time is fulfilled, and the kingdom of God has come near; repent, and believe in the good news.' As Jesus passed along the Sea of Galilee, he saw Simon and his brother Andrew casting a net into the sea—for they were fishermen. And Jesus said to them, 'Follow me and I will make you fish for people.'

Galilee was known at the time of Jesus as 'Galilee of the Gentiles' because this northern section of the ancient land of Israel had been hemmed in by settlements of aliens and, indeed, had been 're-colonized' with Jewish inhabitants under the Roman regime. It surrounds the beautiful lake Galilee and, unusually for such sites, it is truly as beautiful now as ever. The lake is about 13 miles by 8 and surrounded by green hills. It was in this area, where fish and olives provided most of the industry, that Jesus grew up at Nazareth.

Galilee is therefore the setting for all Jesus' early ministry and home to almost all of his disciples. Here we have Mark's typically fast-moving account of the arrival of Jesus on the shores of the lake, fresh from his baptism and time of testing in the wilderness of Judaea.

For Mark, the starting signal for the ministry of Jesus was the arrest of John the Baptist. That was emphatically bad news, but Jesus burst on the scene with the 'good news of God'. That good news was of a moment of destiny that had arrived and of the kingdom of God. To enter into this kingdom, there were two simple things to do—repent and believe.

Simple! 'Repentance'—turning our minds around to admit that God is right and we are wrong—is always one of the most difficult things to do. To believe is to trust—yes, even in dark days, like the moment when a beloved prophet has been snatched away by evil men. It was this hard life to which Jesus now called his first disciples—Simon and Andrew. Yet, 'immediately'—Mark's favourite word—they left their nets and followed Jesus.

Reflection
'Follow me and I will change your life completely.' That was the invitation of Jesus to Simon and Andrew. He certainly did just that…

DW

113

LUKE 2:1–7 (NRSV)

Bethlehem—the house of bread

In those days a decree went out from Emperor Augustus that all the world should be registered. This was the first registration and was taken while Quirinius was governor of Syria. All went to their own towns to be registered. Joseph also went from the town of Nazareth in Galilee to Judea, to the city of David called Bethlehem, because he was descended from the house and family of David. He went to be registered with Mary, to whom he was engaged and who was expecting a child. While they were there, the time came for her to deliver her child. And she gave birth to her firstborn son and wrapped him in bands of cloth, and laid him in a manger, because there was no place for them in the inn.

Thus, Bethlehem—the city of David and, therefore, revered in the history of Israel—became a place of international renown as the birthplace of Jesus. Few towns are more widely known—certainly very few as small as Bethlehem was in the first century or, indeed, until modern times. Its name means 'house of bread'—perhaps it was famous for its bakery at some time in its history!

David came from Bethlehem and, as a boy, kept his sheep on the hills around the town—the hills, presumably, where other shepherds nearly a thousand years later were startled by a vision of angels. Although there was a prophesy that the 'Deliverer' would come from the town (Micah 5:2), Herod seemed unaware of this and needed his scholars to inform him (Matthew 2:3–6). A Roman census—a common event —brought Joseph and Mary back to the town and ensured that the promised Messiah was born there. Later, they returned to Nazareth, to home, family and workshop.

There is something very moving about the way in which God orders events here. When the Son of God is born, it is not in a palace, nor in the city of God, Jerusalem. Instead, he was born in an insignif-icant suburb to a teenage mother, not yet fully married, wrapped in cloths and laid in a feeding trough.

Reflection

In that stable was born the one who would later describe himself as the 'bread of life'. How appropriate, then, that he was born in the 'house of bread'.

DW

Nazareth—the man from nowhere

In the sixth month the angel Gabriel was sent by God to a town in Galilee called Nazareth, to a virgin engaged to a man whose name was Joseph, of the house of David. The virgin's name was Mary. And he came to her and said, 'Greetings, favoured one! The Lord is with you.' But she was much perplexed by his words and pondered what sort of greeting this might be. The angel said to her, 'Do not be afraid, Mary, for you have found favour with God. And now, you will conceive in your womb and bear a son, and you will name him Jesus.'

In that moment, one might say, fame came to Nazareth—the place no one knew of before, Hicksville, Lower Snoring in the Wold, the last place anyone would pick as their home town. Think of Nathanael's sneering comment when he heard where Jesus came from—'Can anything good come out of Nazareth?' (John 1:46). Yet here it is that we see the archangel Gabriel, no less, telling a young peasant woman who was betrothed to the village carpenter in Nazareth that she would be the mother of the Messiah.

So it happened and the Son of God was known on Earth by the title 'Jesus of Nazareth'. Indeed, it was written above his head on the cross in three languages—'Jesus of Nazareth, king of the Jews'. Today, Nazareth is a place of pilgrimage, with a magnificent basilica covering the spot where traditionally Joseph's house was sited and tens of thousands of people flocking with Bibles and cameras and videos to examine the scene—one that is far removed, it must be said, from anything that the boy Jesus would have recognized.

It is somehow consistent with the whole revelation of the nativity that it takes place in the humblest—or perhaps we should say most normal—of situations. Bethlehem, the place of the birth of Jesus, at least had a pedigree: it was the 'city of David'. Nazareth, the place with which history has identified him, had no such distinction. Jesus lived among ordinary working people—not, probably, in grinding poverty, but in a way most people have lived all through human history. When the Word became flesh, it was 'flesh' that we can all recognize.

Prayer

Jesus of Nazareth, son of Mary,
friend of the ordinary and the weak,
have mercy on me.

DW

Bethesda—the place of outpouring

Now in Jerusalem by the Sheep Gate there is a pool... which has five porticoes. In these lay many invalids—blind, lame, and paralysed. One man was there who had been ill for thirty-eight years. When Jesus saw him... he said to him, 'Do you want to be made well?' The sick man answered him, 'Sir, I have no one to put me into the pool when the water is stirred up; and while I am making my way, someone else steps down ahead of me.' Jesus said to him, 'Stand up, take your mat and walk.' At once the man was made well, and he took up his mat and began to walk. Now that day was a sabbath.

Let's disregard the scholarly squabble about its name (some say 'Bethesda', some say 'Beth-zatha') and concentrate on the story. There was a pool in Jerusalem near the sheep gate, its probable site excavated in modern times and the remains of its pillars found. Its fame was its reputation as a place of healing, but the healing only took place when the water was 'stirred' (by an angel, some later manuscripts say). The lame man had waited a long time for healing, but because he had no one to help him to the water, he was always too late.

Jesus required no help in healing him. He simply told him to stand up and pick up his mat, which he did. That should have been the end of the matter, but this happened on the sabbath, when (as some heresy hunters were quick to point out) 'it is not lawful for you to carry your mat' (v. 10). They asked the man who had healed him, but he didn't know the name of his helper (v. 13). Later, Jesus met him in the temple, warning him not to take his healing lightly, 'so that nothing worse happens to you' (v. 14)—solemn words indeed. The man then told the religious teachers that it was Jesus who had healed him and 'the Jews started persecuting Jesus, because he was doing such things on the sabbath' (v. 16). Whatever next?!

Reflection

When the water was stirred, this poor man was always too late to take advantage of it. Is it fanciful to see in this story a reminder that, with Jesus, it is never too late?

DW

Siloam—sent to be blessed

As he walked along, he [Jesus] saw a man blind from birth. His disciples asked him, 'Rabbi, who sinned, this man or his parents, that he was born blind?' Jesus answered, 'Neither this man nor his parents sinned; he was born blind so that God's works might be revealed in him. We must work the works of him who sent me while it is day; night is coming when no one can work. As long as I am in the world, I am the light of the world.' When he had said this, he spat on the ground and made mud with the saliva and spread the mud on the man's eyes, saying to him, 'Go, wash in the pool of Siloam' (which means Sent). Then he went and washed and came back able to see.

The pool of Siloam stood near the walls of Jerusalem opposite the Kidron valley. It was fed by a conduit originally built by Hezekiah (2 Chronicles 32:4) to ensure water supplies in the city during a siege. In the time of Christ, it was primarily a pool for washing and bathing. Perhaps that's why many a Victorian Baptist chapel was named 'Siloam'. Here it becomes the place to which a man blind from birth is 'sent' (the meaning of its name in Hebrew) to wash away the mud with which Jesus had anointed his eyes. Once the washing is complete, the man born blind can see. As Jesus said, 'God's work was revealed in him'. Good news, one would have thought.

Apparently not, however, to the theological splitters of hair, for all this took place, once again, on the sabbath and only 'emergency' healing was permitted then. As a result, the poor man is dragged off for cross-examination. The religious teachers assure him that the man who has done it cannot possibly be from God (John 9:24). The healed man has the perfect, if rather cheeky, riposte to that claim: 'I do not know whether he is a sinner. One thing I do know, that though I was blind, now I see' (v. 25).

Reflection

That was surely the perfect testimony! We may not understand all the doctrines involved, but those whose lives have been touched by Christ do know that they were spiritually blind before, but now they can see.

DW

Damascus road—the decisive moment

Meanwhile Saul, still breathing threats and murder against the disciples of the Lord, went to the high priest and asked him for letters to the synagogues at Damascus, so that if he found any who belonged to the Way, men or women, he might bring them bound to Jerusalem. Now as he was going along and approaching Damascus, suddenly a light from heaven flashed around him. He fell to the ground and heard a voice saying to him, 'Saul, Saul, why do you persecute me?' He asked, 'Who are you, Lord?' The reply came, 'I am Jesus, whom you are persecuting. But get up and enter the city, and you will be told what you are to do.'

Probably most of those who talk about a 'Damascus road experience' have no idea that this was the original version—when Saul of Tarsus, arch scourge of Christians, was stopped in his tracks by the voice of Jesus and a blinding light from the sky. Within a few days, he had been baptized and adopted the name by which he is much more widely known—Paul.

This is held up as the classic 'sudden conversion', but a close reading of the story—both here and as Paul later recounted it—suggests that it wasn't quite as sudden as it seems. Paul later recalled that the voice told him that he was finding it hard to 'kick against the goads' (see 26:14). After he was led into Damascus, he took to prayer (9:11) —for healing, maybe, but more probably (knowing the later Paul), for an explanation.

Saul had been present at the martyrdom of Stephen. Indeed, the executors had 'laid their coats at the feet of a young man named Saul'—his first mention in the New Testament (Acts 7:58). Perhaps he had also been impressed by the demeanour of the Christians he had thrown into prison. The history of Christian conversion suggests that more is usually going on below the surface than that single, split second decision to respond to Christ.

Reflection

What Paul had to do in Damascus was meet a Christian leader called Ananias, be baptized and 'filled with the Holy Spirit' (9:17). What he had to do later was be a chosen 'instrument' of the Lord and 'suffer for the sake of my [Christ's] name' (see vv. 15–16). That really is a 'conversion'.

DW

Luke's parables

'What does it mean, "story"?' asked Matti, aged seven. Matti is Finnish, but he lives in Poland and is educated in English. He speaks Swedish to his father and Russian to his mother. So I explained 'story' as best I could, adding the meaning in Russian. 'I like that word best,' he approved, 'It's the way we say it at home.'

Jesus, too, lived in a multi-lingual society. Aramaic was his mother tongue. Hebrew was the language of the synagogue. Greek was spoken in the marketplace, while the Roman conquerors and their soldiery spoke Latin. Seven Aramaic sayings survive in the Authorized Version of the Bible. When we read the parables of Jesus, however, we are given a unique and very precious hint of 'the way we say it at home.'

A glimpse into their context and cultural setting helps us appreciate the parables more fully. Friends from Africa and Asia have given me insights into life in biblical times. No instant food—it took a long time to kill and cook the fatted calf. Making the mistake once of offering a handshake to a Muslim man, I began to understand a different dimension of human relationships. Marriage is often not a personal decision. In the extended family, people of importance speak first. The head of a household would never hurry, let alone run. It would be completely beneath his dignity—added to which, his long robes would be a hindrance. This led me to a new understanding of the father so prodigal in love that he lowered himself in the eyes of the whole village as he ran along the dusty road to bring his lost son home.

Recent Bible scholarship has examined the intricate literary structure of the parables as well as their context in Middle Eastern village society. That world has changed little since the elders at the gate watched in dismay as the no-good son hurried abroad, cutting himself off from the close-knit community. However, the kingdom of God is organic and open, growing from within, like yeast, like a seed; it challenges limited expectations and lifts despondent hearts. The parables reveal the secrets of the Kingdom, as well as the intellect, courage, compassion and character of the Saviour who set out eternal truths in stories packed with drama, humour and witty word-play, told so memorably that even the simplest can understand.

Jenny Robertson

119

Wonder upon wonder

Then Jesus asked, 'What is the kingdom of God like... It is like a mustard seed, which a man took and planted in his garden. It grew and became a tree, and the birds of the air perched in its branches... It is like yeast that a woman took and mixed into a large amount of flour until it worked all through the dough.'

These two stories (also found in Matthew 13:31–33 and Mark 4:30–32) point up the way Jesus used everyday life to explain the kingdom of God.

The kingdom is organic and secret, ordinary and commonplace, but it transforms the everyday. The process of growth from a hidden seed or leaven is understood by 21st-century biologists, but for the people of Jesus' time, it was a daily marvel. St Brendan, the Irish monk and explorer, said, 'In Christ is wonder upon wonder and every wonder true.' The more we unpack the parables, even the shortest and seemingly simplest, the more marvels we find—so much so that we will take two days to mull over just these two! We'll start with the second one—yeast being mixed into dough.

'Shall I tell you what God's kingdom is like?' Jesus begins. We can imagine an expectant rustle among the listeners. They were going to crack open the deepest theological theory—and all this without going to university! The next words would have drawn nods of agreement. They'd all watched their womenfolk making bread. They knew that dough without yeast was flat and heavy, that the leaven transformed it. Anyone who makes bread will know the fresh smell of yeast and the thrill of watching dough rise. The next words, though, were shocking. Jesus compares the kingdom of God to something a woman does! A woman! Scholars note that in Middle Eastern villages to this day men apologize if they use the word 'woman' in their conversation. Jesus is explicit, however. God's kingdom is for everyone and no one is inferior.

She's making a 'large amount'. I love the generosity of the Gospels. Jesus' listeners are poor, but God's mercy is abundant and permeates the saddest, heaviest parts of our lives like leaven in dough.

Sunday prayer

Transform our lives, Lord, as we worship you today. Fill our churches with the fragrance of your love.

JR

A small seed—a life-giving tree

This is what the Sovereign Lord says: I myself will take a shoot from the very top of a cedar and plant it; I will break off a tender sprig from its topmost shoots and plant it on a high and lofty mountain. On the mountain heights of Israel I will plant it; it will produce branches and bear fruit and become a splendid cedar. Birds of every kind will nest in it; they will find shelter in the shade of its branches.

Ezekiel 17 provides the background for Jesus' parable of the mustard seed in Luke 13:18–19. Jesus, the Living Word, is the 'tender sprig' from the kingly line of David. His teaching, like a fruitful tree, provides shelter and nourishment for Israel, but also for 'birds of every kind'—in other words, for you and me and all the people of the world.

The story puzzled our study group in Warsaw. 'Mustard doesn't grow to any great size', one man rightly objected. However, the size of the mustard tree has been exaggerated on purpose. Exaggeration was expected of a Palestinian storyteller, whose audience appreciated the humour and liked to get the 'big picture'.

Mustard is valued for flavour. In Russia it's used to scour pots or sinks. People take mustard baths to sweat off a fever. As the Roman naturalist Pliny explained, mustard seed is prolific—it can take over an entire garden and is impossible to eradicate. Similarly, Jesus wants his message to spread over the whole world. His kingdom includes everyone. The kingdom of God works secretly, but powerfully, as leaven, producing a 'large amount' of dough, as we read yesterday, and as rampantly as mustard, taking over the world. Yet, there's a twist in the tale. Like those birds, people who belong to the kingdom and rightly enjoy its shelter and sustenance, must also peck away at injustice. The gospel is life-giving and uncompromising.

Finally, fulfilling the beautiful picture in Ezekiel, Jesus engraved this parable indelibly 'in his body on the tree' (1 Peter 2:24). The wooden cross, 'planted' on the hill of death, would become refuge and shelter, healing and salvation for all the nations.

Reflection
Christian mission reaches out, but Christian churches are often self-selecting. Is my church a bird-scarer or an outstretched branch?

JR

A friend in need

Then he [Jesus] said to them, 'Suppose one of you has a friend, and he goes to him at midnight and says, "Friend, lend me three loaves of bread, because a friend of mine on a journey has come to me, and I have nothing to set before him." Then the one inside answers, "Don't bother me. The door is already locked, and my children are with me in bed. I can't get up and give you anything." I tell you... because of the man's boldness he will get up and give him as much as he needs.'

In Scotland, the laws of hospitality were so sacred that the massacre of Glencoe (1692) has remained a scandal because the murderers had come as guests. Macbeth knows that, as Duncan's host, he 'should against his murderer shut the door'. In Slavonic countries, they say, 'A guest in the home—God in the home.' The same is still true in the Middle East, where a slight to a guest is a slur on the honour of the community.

This is the thought behind Jesus' story. A friend arrives at midnight and the family hasn't got enough food to honour him. It would be an insult to offer leftovers. In the context of the village it is unthinkable that the other friend would refuse to get up. His name would be mud throughout the village and, anyway, the host only needs to go next door and ask there. We can imagine the listeners ticking off those feeble excuses and laughing—the very idea would have been nonsense to them. They would know, too, that, although he politely asks for the bare minimum, the host will receive from this house or the next enough for an entire meal—the loaves are merely 'cutlery', broken and dipped into the main course. The whole village will be involved, everyone anxious to share the honour of hosting a guest.

Jesus has just taught the family prayer (vv. 2–4). This parable provides a commentary on the Father's generosity. We're not to imagine a grudging God who won't get up to open the door. Jesus insists that we come to God as guests of an unstinting host who gives us all we need—in fact, 'immeasurably more' (Ephesians 3:20).

Prayer
Father, thank you for our daily bread, for giving us everything we need.

JR

Love your neighbour as yourself

An expert in the law stood up to test Jesus. 'Teacher,' he asked, 'what must I do to inherit eternal life?' 'What is written in the Law?' he replied. 'How do you read it?' He answered: '"Love the Lord your God with all your heart and with all your soul and with all your strength and with all your mind", and "Love your neighbour as yourself."' 'You have answered correctly,' Jesus replied. 'Do this and you will live.'

The 16th-century mystic St John of the Cross wrote, 'There are depths to be fathomed in Christ. He is like a rich mine with many recesses containing treasures, and no matter how men try to fathom them the end is never reached. That is why St Paul said of Christ, "In whom are hidden all the treasures of wisdom and knowledge"' (Colossians 2:3).

An expert stands, respectfully, but asks a loaded question. Jesus' reply draws out the lawyer's understanding of scripture, but then he takes the discussion further. The lawyer is looking for specific situations that he can tick off—'I've done this; I'm all right.' So Jesus gives him one: a wounded man abandoned on a dangerous road (see the next two days' readings).

This story has seven episodes. It is so simple that even the smallest child is gripped by it, yet so profound that we will never come to an end of it. This scriptural, theological reply to a testing question points up two kinds of evil—violent robbery and self-interested neglect. It attacks religious and ethnic prejudices, fearlessly exposing deeply felt hatred. It illustrates the Sermon on the Mount: 'For I tell you that unless your righteousness surpasses that of the Pharisees and the teachers of the Law, you will certainly not enter the kingdom of heaven… Love your enemies… Be perfect, therefore, as your heavenly Father is perfect' (Matthew 5:20, 44, 48). The timeless story demonstrates the love of God who bound up the wounds of his people, pouring out the oil and wine of salvation, sending his Son to rescue the helpless victim, paying the price of the robbery, providing rescue and refuge, not counting the cost.

Reflection

O loving wisdom of our God!
When all was sin and shame,
A second Adam to the fight
And to the rescue came.

John Henry Newman, 1801–90
JR

'Who is my neighbour?'

But he wanted to justify himself, so he asked Jesus, 'And who is my neighbour?' In reply Jesus said: 'A man was going down from Jerusalem to Jericho, when he fell into the hands of robbers. They stripped him of his clothes, beat him, and went away, leaving him half-dead. A priest... saw the man, he passed by on the other side. So too, a Levite, when he came to the place and saw him, passed by on the other side.

The robbers stripped their victim and left him 'half-dead'. The priest dared not go too close to investigate. He wasn't allowed to approach a dead relative, so why risk defilement from a stranger? (Leviticus 21:1–4). He would have to tear his garments and return to the temple, but, instead of standing up at the front, leading the worship, he would have to humbly join inferior, unclean people to be purified. Apocryphal Wisdom counselled, 'Give to the devout, do not go to the help of a sinner' (Ecclesiasticus 12:4, NJB). The priest couldn't tell what kind of man this was. He felt quite justified in 'passing by on the other side'.

The Levite stopped, crossed over, then hurried away.

The present Israeli ambassador to Poland owes his life to a Polish family who hid him in a loft for 18 dangerous months. At a ceremony in Warsaw, he handed awards to elderly Polish people, too frail to mount the steps to the podium, who had rescued Jewish people in World War II. One couple had lived on Twarda (Hard) Street, 'But their hearts were soft,' joked the ambassador, 'They saved five people. Five!' he held up five fingers to show us.

There were tears of joy as a lady met long-lost 'sisters' who had hidden her although her father was executed for rescuing a Jewish child. A toddler was present with his family to receive the award on behalf of dead grandparents—a rich legacy of bravery and goodness. The people honoured had known terror and destruction, shortages and martial law. Today, their pensions scarcely buy basic necessities, but they are the salt of the earth, who refused to 'pass by on the other side', instead risking their lives to help their neighbours.

Prayer

Father, show me my neighbour and help me not to pass by.

JR

The mind of Christ

'But a Samaritan, as he travelled, came where the man was; and... took pity on him. He went to him and bandaged his wounds, pouring on oil and wine. Then he put the man on his own donkey, brought him to an inn and took care of him. The next day he took out two silver coins and gave them to the innkeeper... Which of these three do you think was a neighbour to the man who fell into the hands of robbers?' The expert in the law replied, 'The one who had mercy on him.' Jesus told him, 'Go and do likewise.'

Four years ago, Wladyslaw Szpilman's book *The Pianist* took Germany by storm. At death's door in burning Warsaw, Jewish Szpilman had been rescued by a German. When his book was first published in Poland in 1946, the authorities withdrew it at once. It was simply not permissible to say anything positive about a German officer.

Perhaps this helps us to see how Jesus' story challenges prejudice and hatred. Having heard about the priest and Levite, the crowd would expect that the next traveller might take a risk and help the wounded man. They would certainly expect the unselfish rescuer to be one of their own, a Jew. Instead, with outstanding moral courage, Jesus makes the man who shows mercy a hated Samaritan.

He, too, is at risk from the robbers, but he stops, dismounts, comes across to the man, pours out oil and wine from his own supplies and binds up the wounds. The language is simple, the actions are dramatic, but, as we saw on Wednesday, this parable is a theological statement about God's loving kindness and salvation. The Lord 'will heal us... he will bind up our wounds', says Hosea (6:1). The Samaritan puts the wounded man on his own donkey and walks, like a servant, to the nearest inn, where he takes care of him, paying the innkeeper generously, restoring to the man everything the robbers have taken—health, status and property. Confronted with this startling truth, the lawyer, evasively and grudgingly answers Jesus' question. Jesus tells him, as he tells us, 'Go and do likewise.'

Reflection
'Your attitude should be the same as that of Christ Jesus: who... made himself nothing... and became obedient to death.'
(Philippians 2:5–8, abridged).

JR

Waiting on God

Be dressed ready for service and keep your lamps burning, like men waiting for their master to return from a wedding banquet, so that when he comes and knocks they can immediately open the door for him. It will be good for those servants whose master finds them watching when he comes. I tell you the truth, he will dress himself to serve, will have them recline at the table and will come and wait on them.

Like the Good Samaritan, this short story has an elaborate construction of seven sections and a theological message. The last section is introduced by emphatic words used six times in Luke's Gospel—'I tell you the truth.' This truth is shocking: the master will wait on the servants.

There's a surprise for modern readers in the third section, too. There's this great build-up of preparation and readiness. The servants have tucked up their long robes, 'ready for service'. Their lamps are trimmed and filled with oil, but they are not doing anything. They are just waiting. What a frustrating waste of time and energy!

In Rudyard Kipling's children's novel *Puck of Pook's Hill*, Brother Hugh asks, 'Then we do nothing?' 'We wait,' replies De Aquila, and adds, 'I am old, but still I find that the most grievous work I know.'

Waiting is never easy for people geared for action. It goes against the grain. Bernard of Clairvaux called it the greatest work there is. Waiting can be fruitful, however. Prayerful waiting ploughs the heart so that the seeds of God are deeply sown. The Holy Spirit works when we wait, as we see in Acts 1:14: 'They all joined together constantly in prayer…' It was then that the Holy Spirit swept through the place with fire and power.

Jesus stresses the value of attentive waiting. Those who are prepared to be servants, attentive and alert, waiting for God to work, will be served by the one for whom they wait. The master will discard his festive robe, make the servants recline and will serve them—as Jesus himself does when he washes his disciples' feet (John 13:4–5). Such role reversal was unheard of and unthinkable, but Jesus did it all the same.

Reflection

'They that wait upon the Lord shall renew their strength'
(Isaiah 40:31, KJV).

JR

The banquet is ready—come!

Jesus replied: 'A certain man was preparing a great banquet and invited many guests. At the time of the banquet he sent his servant to tell those who had been invited, 'Come, for everything is now ready.' But they all alike began to make excuses... Then the owner of the house became angry and ordered his servant, 'Go out quickly into the streets and alleys of the town and bring in the poor, the crippled, the blind and the lame... so that my house will be full.'

If you have time, you may like to read verses 1–23 in full. The story has seven speeches and is set within the context of a sabbath meal (Luke 14:1). Jesus heals a sick man (vv. 2–6). Some guests pick the best seats and Jesus tells a parable in reply (vv. 7–11). He also says we should invite people who cannot invite us back (vv. 12–14). A guest responds with a safe, religious-sounding remark (v. 15) that sparks off the parable.

Sundays can be so busy that we often don't have time to read anything in full! Sometimes we have to strike a balance between being open to others and having time for ourselves, but the parables of Jesus encourage us to err on the side of generosity. I've always appreciated the love so many Christians show when they invite strangers or misfits into the family circle. Friends in Warsaw set us an outstanding example. Their invitations to dinner included broken, lonely people along with family members, top scientists and diplomats. Table fellowship is a precious thing. As Jesus said in this very parable, 'Bring them all in.' 'Anyone welcome', as a little girl wrote on a church invitation.

In a hot country without freezers, animals once killed had to be cooked and eaten immediately. So, the invitations went out first and then the servant announced that supper was ready. At this point, the story takes its kingdom shape. God's grace is undeserved and can never be reciprocated. It is costly as the host lays himself open to rejection. The guests turned down his invitation, insulting their host with feeble excuses, so outcasts and outsiders were invited instead.

Sundy prayer

Lord, thank you that your great banquet includes me. May our churches be places for the poor and the lame and may our worship today be a feast of praise.

JR

The prayer that sets us free

To some who were confident of their own righteousness and looked down on everybody else, Jesus told this parable: 'Two men went up to the temple to pray, one a Pharisee and the other a tax collector. The Pharisee stood up and prayed about himself... But the tax collector stood at a distance. He would not even look up to heaven, but beat his breast and said, "God, have mercy on me, a sinner"'.

A district nurse doing Sunday shifts tended an old woman who'd 'worked' the docks for years. Her home was unbelievably squalid and her common-law husband abused and terrorized her. As the nurse left, gratefully breathing in fresh air, people across the road were spilling out of church. The contrast couldn't have been greater and she often wondered what the couple that so desperately needed God would make of the worship in church or how the people in that church would receive them if they entered its doors.

Jesus takes an extreme example like this in his story of two men in the temple. Two thousand years later, we still hear the scorn when the Pharisee says, 'I thank you that I am not like other men... or even like this tax collector' (v. 11). His prayer is only about himself. His worship simply adds to his sense of self-satisfaction and, as a result, he goes away as empty and puffed up as he came. The tax collector, however, bows down in deep remorse,

beats his chest in extreme anguish and cries out for mercy.

The scene is set in the temple, where sacrifices for sin were offered. Although the tax collector is standing 'at a distance' (v. 13), he longs for cleansing and forgiveness. He has nothing to offer and so casts himself entirely on God's mercy.

Jesus isn't advocating false humility. He highlights the danger of being so self-satisfied that we have no room in our hearts for God. His story explains the true meaning of prayer and worship, which is that mercy and grace are freely given when we trust in God and not in our status. For, says Jesus, the tax collector's prayer was answered: he walked away free (v. 14).

Prayer

The tax collector's words are enshrined in Christian tradition as the Jesus Prayer. Let's echo them today and pray, Lord Jesus Christ, have mercy on me, a sinner.

JR

Real estate

Then he said to them, 'Watch out! Be on your guard against all kinds of greed; a man's life does not consist in the abundance of his possessions... The ground of a certain rich man produced a good crop. He thought to himself, "What shall I do? I have no place to store my crops." Then he said, "This is what I'll do. I will tear down my barns and build bigger ones... eat, drink and be merry." But God said to him, "You fool! This very night your life will be demanded from you." Then who will get what you have prepared for yourself?'

As so often, Jesus' parable is told in response to a question. A man demands, 'Give me my rights!' (v. 13). Jesus refuses to take sides. Instead, he leads the discussion to a deeper level.

The teaching he offers the disciples at the end of the story explains what he means (vv. 22–34). It's important to note that Jesus isn't talking against riches, but against greed. That's why he says that we matter more than birds (v. 24). The Father himself provides for us. We are the Father's 'little flock' (v. 32) as richly clad as lilies (v. 27). So, what more do we need? A lot, alas, it seems. This parable is particularly hard-hitting when it is told in rich countries where governments protect their economic levels, usually at the expense of the poor.

I live in a city with much obvious wealth amid hardship. The rich guard their property with high fences, security men or ferocious dogs. The price of affluence is loneliness and isolation. In this parable, the friendless rich man talks to himself alone. Like the Pharisee in yesterday's reading, his thoughts are all 'me'. God speaks directly to him at this point in the strongest possible language (v. 20).

In many parables, the real meaning is hidden, but there's no beating about the bush in this one. The very fact that Jesus quotes God's words shows how serious the sin of greed is. The final words 'for yourself' cut through to the heart of this particular sin with devastating accuracy. The man who has piled up material goods has lived only for himself, not for his family, nor for others in the community, nor for the poor and certainly not for God.

Reflection
Let me be open-handed and God-directed.

JR

Manifold and great mercies

Jesus told his disciples: 'There was a rich man whose manager was accused of wasting his possessions. So he called him in... "Give an account of your management, because you cannot be manager any longer." The manager said to himself, "What shall I do now? My master is taking away my job..." So he called in each of his master's debtors. He asked the first, "How much do you owe my master?" "Eight hundred gallons of olive oil", he replied. The manager told him, "Take your bill, sit down quickly and make it 400"... The master commended the dishonest manager because he had acted shrewdly...'

This story has always puzzled me. I could never work out why the master praised his dishonest manager at the end of the story. Gradually, though, I understood that the crux of the story is the mercy of the master. Although he rightly dismisses the manager, he doesn't punish him in any way. The normal thing would be to have him flung in jail. After all, the man he has trusted has squandered large amounts of his wealth. Moreover, the sacked steward still has access to the account books.

However, he's in a mess. His CV is none too good. He can't sponge off people indefinitely, yet, if the community doesn't feed him, he'll starve. So, quickly, before word gets round that he's been sacked, he calls in his master's debtors and cuts their debts. The good news would be gossiped around in no time. 'What a generous master! How kind and merciful he is', the debtors would tell their families and neighbours. We already know that this is true. The master is generous—he hasn't jailed his manager. The manager stakes his crafty plan on the master's generosity and mercy—and the master does not let him down. He bears the cost of the manager's dishonesty.

Here is the gospel in a nutshell. God's mercy covers all the costs of my failure and sin. He bears the cost of my transgressions. Notice that the story is addressed directly to the disciples (v. 1). So, says Jesus, if an estate owner behaves this generously, how much more can we throw ourselves completely and confidently on God's mercy.

Prayer

Not trusting in our own righteousness, but in your manifold and great mercies.

JR

Unworthy servants

Suppose one of you had a servant ploughing or looking after the sheep. Would he say to the servant when he comes in from the field, 'Come along now and sit down to eat'? Would he not rather say, 'Prepare my supper, get yourself ready and wait on me while I eat and drink; after that you may eat and drink'?... So you also, when you have done everything you were told to do, should say, 'We are unworthy servants; we have only done our duty.'

Jesus told a story about servants faithfully waiting for their master's return, whom the master would then serve (Luke 12:35–37, see 21 August). Today's parable seems a complete reversal of this. It seems, too, to contradict the generosity, mercy and costly grace that runs like a golden thread through the stories we've been reading. Does Jesus, the Servant King, not say of himself, 'I am among you as one who serves' (Luke 22:27)? Yes, indeed, but he is still Lord. 'You call me "Teacher" and "Lord", and rightly so', he says, taking his place after washing the disciples' feet (John 13:13).

Today's short parable illustrates the response of servants who owe everything to their master. The word 'unworthy' isn't about eating humble pie. The servants are saying, 'We are your slaves. You have provided everything we need. We don't lack anything.' The thought here takes us straight to Psalm 23. I lack nothing because the Lord, my Shepherd, cares for me so abundantly, 'He makes me lie down in green pastures, he leads me beside quiet waters' (v. 2), or, as the Lord himself tells Paul, 'My grace is sufficient for you' (2 Corinthians 12:9).

The servants demonstrate loving trust in their master (Luke 17:10). They are grateful, and gratitude, too, is grace. They speak with a very different voice from the grudging elder brother whose complaints we shall hear next Tuesday (Luke 15:25–32). They are totally unlike the self-righteous Pharisee we met in last Monday's reading (Luke 18:11), but the tax collector who prayed for mercy and went home justified would echo the servants' response to their lord (18:14).

Prayer

*Lord, you have forgiven me every-
thing. Therefore, let me serve you
with a grateful heart and never
expect you to stand and wait on me.*

JR

The lost sheep and the Good Shepherd

Now the tax collectors and 'sinners' were all gathering round to hear him. But the Pharisees and the teachers of the law muttered, 'This man welcomes sinners and eats with them.' Then Jesus told them this parable: Suppose one of you has a hundred sheep and loses one of them. Does he not leave the ninety-nine in the open country and go after the lost sheep until he finds it?'

Complaints and criticisms spark off three stories about being lost and found. First, a shepherd seeks his lost sheep. It's a story that the youngest child can understand, yet it makes a profound statement of redemption: the Good Shepherd bore our sins on his shoulders as he carried the cross to Calvary. The audience, both 'sinners' and 'righteous', know that Moses was a shepherd (Exodus 3:1). David the shepherd-king rejoiced in the Lord, his Shepherd (1 Samuel 16:11, Psalm 23). All Israel knows that 'we are the people of his pasture' (Psalm 95:7). Ezekiel 34 develops that theme. By Jesus' day, however, shepherds didn't have a positive image and his opening words challenged the religious teachers.

What about the 99 left in the wilderness? Probably a large flock had other shepherds to bring them safely home, but, the fact is, we don't know what happened to them, just as we don't know whether or not the elder brother will join the party (Luke 15:32).

With deliberate irony, Jesus links the 99 sheep with the '99 righteous persons who do not need to repent' (v. 7), but, 'there is no-one righteous, not even one' (Romans 3:10). Jesus doesn't need to remind his listeners of Ezekiel 34:15–16: 'I myself will tend my sheep... I will bind up the injured and strengthen the weak, but the sleek and the strong I will destroy. I will shepherd the flock with justice'. If God is like that, the religious teachers, too, should seek the lost and restore them to the fold.

Reflection

Christ is abroad in the world—in the structure of all society, in the dark city streets, in the silent places of man's loneliness and his despair; and there he summons his Church to reflect his love and the coming of his kingdom.

Reverend Geoff Shaw, Iona Community
JR

A woman's quest

Or suppose a woman has ten silver coins and loses one. Does she not light a lamp, sweep the house and search carefully until she finds it? And when she finds it, she calls her friends and neighbours together and says, 'Rejoice with me; I have found my lost coin.' In the same way, I tell you, there is rejoicing in the presence of the angels of God over one sinner who repents.

'Suppose a woman…' The religious teachers had already been shocked by the first story, which linked shepherding to the mission of God, but now a woman?

We've already seen how startling it was for a woman's work to be compared to the growth of the kingdom of God (15 August). Now the woman's search is equated with God's costly mission to the lost. If the Good Shepherd is a picture of our loving God, why not the woman with her broom? Once again, Jesus exposes his listeners' deep-seated prejudice— and sweeps it aside!

The worth of the lost thing increases. With the shepherd, it was one sheep out of a hundred, now it is one coin out of ten. In a village, money rarely changed hands. The coins are the woman's personal insurance against penury and therefore of enormous worth. The scene has shifted from the wilderness to the narrow confines of a windowless house with its earthen floor, but the search is just as strenuous. The woman has to light the lamp and burn precious oil. She has to sweep into all the corners, carefully sifting through loose earth. She has to leave her bread unbaked, her lentils uncooked, her weaving undone.

When she finds the lost coin, her joy is so great that she has to share the good news. The Christian community should be like this, too, says Jesus. Light the lamps of the Spirit, get into action with the brisk broom of the word and keep on hunting until you find the precious thing that was lost. The result is pure joy. Heaven is glad and angels sing.

Like the lost sheep, the coin can do nothing to help itself—both are lost and found, picked up and restored to their proper place.

Reflection
Amazing grace!

JR

Lost... and found!

Jesus continued: 'There was a man who had two sons. The younger one... got together all he had, set off for a distant country and there squandered his wealth in wild living... When he came to his senses he said... "I will set out and go back to my father and say to him: Father, I have sinned against heaven and against you. I am no longer worthy to be called your son; make me like one of your hired men." So he got up and went to his father.'

The village watched him go, the elders at the gate sorrowfully shook grey beards. They had seen too many younger sons leave. Many Galilean farmers lived at bare subsistence level and their land was shared between too many sons. The youngest often inherited nothing and had to seek work as hired hands or go to the city with its temptations and dangers, slipping further away from the requirements of the Law until you could no longer count them as sons of Abraham. There would have been younger sons among the 'sinners' at table with Jesus.

We can imagine a hiss of indignation. 'We never did a thing like that! Poverty forced us off our land, but that young scoundrel as good as stole his inheritance. That's like saying he wished the old man were dead. What did the elder brother do? Nothing, it seems. He should have taken his father's part and given his brother a good whipping. What a servile heart he has! One thing's sure, that lad will come to no good.'

They were right—and wrong. Things turned sour for the younger son, but, when he finally comes to his senses, he comes into very great good. He limps home, rehearsing his confession, imposing his own conditions—he'll get himself back on his feet, he'll be independent, he won't need to live from his father's generosity or seek reconciliation with his brother. His choice is to be a servant, not a son. He neither expects nor needs grace, but, when he was still far off... That is tomorrow's story!

Sunday reflection

Father of all, we give you thanks and praise, that when we were still far off you met us in your Son and brought us home.

Common Worship

JR

Unconditional love

But while he was still a long way off, his father saw him and was filled with compassion for him; he ran to his son, threw his arms around him and kissed him. The son said to him, 'Father, I have sinned against heaven and against you. I am no longer worthy to be called your son.' But the father said to his servants, 'Quick! Bring the best robe and put it on him. Put a ring on his finger and sandals on his feet. Bring the fattened calf and kill it. Let's have a feast and celebrate! For this son of mine... was lost and is found.'

When I shared this parable with a youth group in a well-off area someone quipped, 'The moral is—never leave home without your credit card.' Children I taught in Russia explored the literary structure and cultural background. They painted pictures, wrote newspaper reports, radio interviews and, finally, a play. We lived with this story for a whole term as the Russian winter gave way to spring. The children, whose faces were pale after a long winter and the Lenten fast, entered into the deep heart of the story. 'I love my son,' one child wrote in her retelling, 'I wanted to be the first to meet him.'

The heart of this story is the father who saw his son when he was still a long way off and ran to meet him. We can imagine him on the flat roof, peering along the empty road until the distant, limping figure comes into view. His father heart recognizes the lonely traveller. He throws his dignity to the winds, hoists up his robes and runs along the dusty road.

By the conventions of the day, even if he has been merciful enough to receive a son who has dishonoured the family, it is enough to send a servant, bid the son to wash and change and only then come before his father. This father, though, obeys no conventions except compassion. He hears half his son's confession, but sweeps the self-imposed conditions away. 'We had to celebrate', he tells his grudging elder son afterwards (v. 32). Note 'Had to'! There is only one compulsion: love.

Reflection

*Forgiveness, generosity, grace—
all these come from God and
are what God is.*

JR

A brother outside

Meanwhile, the older son was in the field. When he came near the house, he heard music and dancing... The older brother became angry and refused to go in. So his father went out and pleaded with him. But he answered his father, 'Look! All these years I've slaved for you and never disobeyed your orders. Yet you never gave me even a young goat... But when this son of yours who has squandered your property with prostitutes comes home, you kill the fattened calf for him!' 'My son,' the father said, '... everything I have is yours. But we had to celebrate and be glad, because this brother of yours was dead and is alive again...'

The lost son has come home, but the elder brother is far from happy. His jealousy and anger sour the story and he boycotts the party. However badly he feels about his brother's return, he should have put on his best clothes and best smile. The table is groaning with food and the whole community is invited. So, in full view of his guests, the father leaves the top table, goes outside and pleads with his son—another unheard-of thing. This action equals the love he lavishes on the younger brother —reinstating him in the family, giving him sandals of sonship, a robe of honour, ring of authority and lavish party. All this is Bible shorthand for the generosity of grace. It is Jesus' response to mean-spirited critics who draw a sharp line between sinners and the righteous—themselves.

The elder son's harsh criticisms echo those of the Pharisees. He reveals the grudging heart of a petty servant and is just as undeserving of his father's love as his brother was. Patiently, the father answers the young man's scornful insults with gentle words.

So the story ends... or does it? This wonderful parable is perfectly balanced, but the ending is missing. Does the elder brother join the celebration? The children in St Petersburg found a wise, sensitive answer: 'It is our family secret', they said. One day, when all our stories end, the real one begins at the heavenly banquet and we will know the answer to this and to all our questions.

Prayer

'Everything I have is yours.'
Thank you, dearest Lord.

JR

New Daylight

Magazine

Word for the world:
the work of Media Associates International   138
Pat Alexander

Summer reading—an extract from:
Song of the Shepherd by Tony Horsfall   142

Recommended reading
Growing Leaders by James Lawrence   148

The People's Bible Commentary
Extract from *Proverbs* by Enid Mellor   150

For reflection: *Confessions*   152
Augustine of Hippo

Order forms

Supporting BRF's Ministry   155

Bible Reading Resources Pack   157

Subscriptions   158

BRF Publications   159

Words for the world: the work of Media Associates International

Pat Alexander

Imagine going into your local bookshop. You begin to browse, but something is wrong. The names sound odd and the examples all come from far away. You can't find a single book written by an author from your own country!

In many areas all over Asia, Eastern Europe, Africa and Latin America, less than ten per cent of the Christian material on the shelves comes from local writers who understand the culture and know at first hand the issues people struggle with. Readers look for something that really speaks to them, but all too often it's simply not there.

Working for change

Media Associates International—MAI—was set up in 1985 to help local publishers change all that. It is a small organization, a registered charity in the United States, where it began, and also in Britain as MAI-Europe.

Requests come in from Christian organizations around the world for help in acquiring publishing skills to enable them to produce Christian materials—books, journals and magazines—for their own people, reflecting their own culture.

MAI exists to equip talented men and women for this task, and has developed an international network of trainers who are able to share their skills and experience of writing, editing and the whole business of publishing in a culturally sensitive way.

Sharing skills and expertise

Help is concentrated on the neediest areas. Interactive workshops are arranged at the request of nationals in the countries concerned. MAI matches individual trainers to the need and agrees a programme with the host group. They may want specific training for writers, editors or designers, or to learn more about publishing as a business, about promotion, marketing and sales. It is this emphasis on going to the places where the need is, sharing and supporting, which makes MAI's work so special and so effective.

To give a personal example, in May 2000 I was asked to go to Albania to help lead the first ever workshop there for Christian writers and editors. I went with MAI's director, John Maust, at the invitation of Besa Shapllo, a remarkable Albanian woman who produces *Miracle*, a magazine for children which sells into all the schools, with state approval—astonishing in view of the fact that Albania was an atheist state until 1990.

Two years later, in June 2002, I was in Albania again, sharing the teaching with three talented Albanians now ready and able to take the lead in a second workshop. This time, even more than before, I was learning from others as well as sharing my own publishing experience. One session was led by Ledia Ikonomi, who came to the first workshop as a student, and was now about to become the editor of *Miracle* magazine. It is exciting to see how quickly talented young people like Ledia can grow and progress.

In April 2003 Ledia came to a conference in Austria to further equip her to train others. When she got home she wrote to John Maust: 'Thank you for inviting me to Mittersill. I had a very good experience… I never felt uncomfortable even that I was the youngest. I had many questions on my mind before I came there, and now I have the answers, not only for my work here in Tirana, but answers about my life. During the workshop I found myself in a real family.' Many others in the MAI network express that same feeling of family.

LITT-WORLD

Once every two years MAI brings together about 150 contacts from some 40 countries for the LITT-WORLD conference. The next one takes place in November. For the second time it will be held at a conference centre outside Manila, in the Philippines. These conferences are a very important part of MAI's work, giving inspiration and practical help to people who are often isolated and discouraged.

LITT-WORLD was a memorable experience

After LITT-WORLD 2002, writer and editor Roshini Wickremesinghe wrote: 'LITT-WORLD was a memorable experience; a combination of learning, sharing, fellowship and laughter. I returned to Sri Lanka encouraged, inspired and with a wonderful feeling of having been hugged by the wider family of God… it is so nice to know that I am not alone!'

Many of those who apply to come—who would bring most to it and gain most from it—need help with travel and accommodation costs which are way beyond their means, though all contribute something. MAI's resources are slender and gifts of money from individuals and organizations are needed to fund scholarships. These gifts all help someone to return encouraged and better equipped for the work in their own country. In a world where it is crucial for Christian values to be brought to people through local, culturally-specific books and magazines, this is a very strategic need.

Building relationships

What's special about LITT-WORLD is not so much the addresses, excellent as they are, but the number of small-group interactive sessions on a whole range of practical subjects. About 40 of the delegates are involved in these groups as resource leaders. There are one-to-one 'clinics', too, where individuals can consult a leader about particular problems or questions.

'Attending LITT-WORLD was the best thing that has happened to me within Christian publishing,' wrote Annabel Tan, managing editor of *Compass* magazine in Singapore after LITT-WORLD 2002. 'What was really encouraging was the spirit of humility and sharing evidenced by each key leader present. You would see a resource leader teaching at one session— and the very next moment he or she would be sitting in another session learning from others!'

Besides new skills and vision gained from the conference, an important benefit of LITT-WORLD 2000 came through new relationships and networking between participants from six continents.

'LITT-WORLD was an opportunity to meet and connect with other Christian print-media professionals from around the world,' said David Waweru of Cana Publishing in Kenya.

Kenyan writer Wambura Kiminyu added, 'LITT-WORLD brings together people who believe that they can change their world through words. When I attend LITT-WORLD, I am reminded that dreams know no colour, gender, race, culture or political, social or sectional inclination.'

How MAI has helped

These are some instances of help given through the dozen or so workshops and training sessions which take place each year, and in other ways. MAI has:

• provided publisher and author training for Bookprint Creative Services in Nairobi, Kenya.
• conducted a three-year editor and author training programme for a start-up Christian publishing house in Venezuela.
• arranged publishing internships for staff from Sierra Leone, Burkina Faso, Poland, Argentina, Hong Kong and Mexico.
• led an editorial training seminar for Christian publishers in the Balkans.
• published a series of 'author journey' books featuring Christian writers from Africa, Asia and Latin America.

It's all about people

This work is all about people. So let me tell you just a little about some other members of the MAI family and the work in which they are involved.

Lawrence Darmani won a Commonwealth prize for his first novel, *Grief Child*. He publishes two successful Christian magazines in Ghana and is one of MAI's most enthusiastic and successful trainers.

Femi Cakolli from Pristina came to the first MAI writers' workshop in Albania and returned two years later as a leader. He managed to get his magazine on the newsstands around the country within days of the end of the war in Kosova. How? Femi's graphic designer slipped the computer hard drive into his pocket as he fled for the Albanian border. Once there, he continued working so that the issue was ready for printing as soon as the fighting ended.

Nelson Clemens has recently relaunched his magazine *Catalyst* in war-torn Sierra Leone. It addresses tough issues. 'I am committed to making whatever contribution God will allow and enable me to make for the restoration of our nation,' Nelson writes.

Ramon Rocha, a successful businessman who is now publisher of OMF literature in the Philippines, hosted LITT-WORLD 2002 and will also host the coming conference. After a training workshop Ramon wrote, 'We thank God for the valuable training and ideas you shared with us. It will be exciting to see how Christian publishing in the Philippines will improve as a result of the Editorial Training Conference.' Ramon is now committed to help with print-media training in other Asian countries.

As the author of the letter to the Hebrews put it, 'Time is too short for me to tell'... of Joanna Ilboudo in Burkina Faso, George Koshy in India, Alina Wieja in Poland, and so many more. It is a very special privilege to know, work with and support people like these; humbling, too, to learn of the difficulties they have to face and overcome. We have so many Christian books available to us in our own country. We surely owe something to those who have so much less.

Pat Alexander is co-founder and former Editorial Director of Lion Publishing and a Trustee for MAI-Europe and member of MAI's Board of Directors.

You can learn more about MAI's training programme on its web site: www.littworld.org. If you would like to sponsor a LITT-WORLD conference participant from a needy area of the world, please contact MAI-Europe, Concorde House, Grenville Place, Mill Hill, London NW7 3SA; email: MAIEurope@aol.com.

If you would like your name on the mailing list to receive MAI's quarterly newsletter, Profile, contact Pat Alexander direct by e-mail: patalexander@mac.com

An extract from
Song of the Shepherd

Of all the psalms written by King David, the most popular and well-known is Psalm 23, yet its very familiarity may lead us to miss its beauty and fail to hear its message. *Song of the Shepherd* shows that the picture of the loving shepherd and his sheep speaks profoundly about how we can relate to God. Author Tony Horsfall examines the psalm verse by verse, covering key discipleship issues for both new and mature Christians—learning how to rest in God, how to trust him through difficult times, how to live from the resources he provides.

The divine companion

Sheep seem to have an instinctive awareness of the presence of their shepherd. If they can see him or hear the sound of his voice, they are secure and at peace. Without him they become anxious and nervous. When passing through dark and frightening places, it is essential, therefore, that they know he is with them. The shepherd does his best to let them know he is there, walking among them, calling out to them and making himself both seen and heard.

What sustains us through the hard times in life? It is that same sense of the presence of the good Shepherd. It has been said that that presence is the antidote to fear, and certainly the conscious awareness that God is with us is essential if we are to cope with the feelings of anxiety and worry that threaten to engulf us in our moments of darkness. 'For you are with me' is a certainty born out of David's own nightmare experiences of abandonment and betrayal, of humiliating flight and heart-stopping moments. It is a promise on which every trusting believer must learn to depend.

Many commentators draw attention to the change in pronouns at this point in the psalm. The more impersonal 'he' suddenly becomes the more intimate 'you', as if the thought of the valley and its difficulty reminds David of the closeness to God that can be experienced at such times. It is a strange thing, but adversity has its way of bringing us nearer to God and making us more aware of his presence. This is one of the main blessings of such moments, and helps us to understand a little of why God allows us to go through such experiences.

I know there are some for whom the valley of deep darkness means the loss of all conscious awareness of God. It involves what St John of the Cross called the 'dark night of the soul', when a person seems unable to apprehend God at all, even though they formerly experienced his presence constantly. They feel abandoned, aware only of dryness and emptiness and an aching hunger for God. Such experiences have been written about for centuries in the classics of spiritual literature, and some would say that such periods are part of a necessary passage in spiritual transformation, bringing us to the end of one phase of knowing God and opening up for us new ways of relating to him. They can perhaps be described as 'the Easter Saturday of the soul', that time of waiting in the darkness between the end of one thing (the death of Good Friday) and the beginning of another (the resurrection of Easter Sunday).

For others, the darkness of the valley speaks of the depression and mental anguish that they experience almost continually. Life for them really is like passing through a valley of deep gloom from which there is little relief. All of us have periods of slight depression, but these are soon over. For a few people, the gloom never seems to lift. Ian Barclay, in *He is Everything to Me,* devotes a whole chapter to this subject, citing many well-known Christians who have battled with depression. It is said that in Britain, for example, one out of every ten people will suffer from mental illness at some time in their life. It is inevitable, therefore, that some Christians will face this particular form of darkness. By reason of their personality and make-up they seem more prone to depression.

There are some for whom the valley of deep darkness means the loss of all conscious awareness of God

While validating the reality of both the dark night of the soul and the darkness that is depression, it is important to say that neither is to be the norm. It is only our apprehension of God's presence that is affected in such seasons. Whether we are aware of it or not, God is still present with us, for it is impossible for him to abandon his people. The reason that Jesus experienced the horror of God-forsakenness on the cross was so that we might never know what it is to be abandoned by him. His agonized cry, 'My God, my God, why have you forsaken me?' (Matthew 27:46) means that he endured that awful abandonment so that we do not have to. On a cloudy day, when we do not see the sun, we do not conclude that it has ceased to exist or stopped shining, simply because we do not feel its presence. We know that, hidden from our eyes behind the clouds, the sun shines as brightly as ever. Likewise, faith dares to believe that even when there is no emotional awareness of God's presence, he is still with us, shining his love upon us in faithful consistency.

Unseen, often unfelt, the God who cannot abandon us is always close by. Though he may appear to hide himself for a time, in the end his presence will break forth into our lives again like the sun in the morning. And even when he seems far off, his gracious influence is still at work in our lives, sustaining and keeping us, imparting to us strength we never knew we had. The good Shepherd will never abandon his sheep. We learn to walk by faith, not by sight, and to trust in the reliability of his prom-

ise and the faithfulness of his character.

The promise of our shepherding God is that he will never leave us or forsake us. Through the prophet Isaiah he gave this assurance: 'When you pass through the waters, I will be with you; and when you pass through the rivers, they will not sweep over you. When you walk through the fire, you will not be burned; the flames will not set you ablaze. For I am the Lord your God' (Isaiah 43:2–3). Whether facing floods or fires (or any other calamity in life), he is there to lead and guide us.

The writer to the Hebrews takes hold of a similar assurance to remind his readers of a promise first given to Israel as they entered the promised land. 'Never will I leave you; never will I forsake you' (Hebrews 13:5). THE MESSAGE translates this in its own punchy style as 'I'll never let you down, never walk off and leave you.' A more literal expression draws out the negatives in the original Greek that make it even more emphatic: 'I will never leave you nor forsake you, not never, no-how'. Trust involves taking hold of such promises as these, and hanging on to them until we are

Unseen, often unfelt, the God who cannot abandon us is always close by

through the valley. We need to believe that God is as good as his word.

The greatest reassurance of all, however, comes through our awareness that, in Jesus, God has stepped into our world and lived our life. Far from abandoning us, he became one of us, entering our world of time and space, taking human form and experiencing its joys and its sorrows. He became Emmanuel, God with us. In sharing our humanity, he is able now to serve as a merciful and faithful high priest on our behalf, not only interceding for us but pouring his sustaining grace on our lives. We are not alone in the valley, for he comes to us again and again in our need as our Emmanuel, the ever-present helper in time of need.

This was Paul's experience. At one of the lowest points in his life, he felt that everyone had deserted him. Arrested and put on trial for his faith, no one came to help him; everyone abandoned him. 'But the Lord stood at my side,' he writes, 'and gave me strength' (2 Timothy 4:16–17). Dark as his circumstances were, and bleak as his future must have looked, he found himself wrapped in the divine presence. The Shepherd was watching over him.

Nor was it the first time that the great apostle had needed to know the reassurance of the divine presence. It had happened years before in Corinth, when opposition to his preaching was strong, and inside he felt lonely and afraid. One night God spoke to him in a vision. 'Do not be afraid; keep on speaking, do not be silent. For I am with you, and no one is going to attack and harm you, because I have many people in this city' (Acts 18:9–10). Just when he needed it most, reassurance came. In the darkness, light began to shine. Strengthened inside, he was able to continue his ministry and cope with its pressures.

Such supernatural occurrences are quite rare in my experience. Usually the presence of God is communicated to us in an inexplicable awareness of his nearness, an intuitive sense that he is there. It cannot be explained in rational terms; it is an intuitive knowledge beyond words, but real nonetheless. It may come in a sudden experience of peace, or in a deep-seated awareness of a quiet joy filling our hearts. Occasionally

> *Far from abandoning us, he became one of us, entering our world of time and space*

it is experienced as a simple knowledge that all is going to be well, or as the ability to relax in the midst of turmoil. God draws near to us and we feel his presence. Perhaps most often, though, it comes to us fleshed out in the love and concern of others, the spoken words and caring actions that remind us that God has not left us.

Dr Leslie Weatherhead, the famous Methodist minister, was once called to visit a woman whose husband had died suddenly and tragically. Friends had gathered to comfort her and sat with her as she spoke to the minister. 'Where's God in this?' she asked accusingly. Weatherhead thought for a moment, then pointed to one of the friends sitting close by with her arm around the woman. 'I think he's there,' he said quietly, 'in the comfort of your friend.'

Perhaps sometimes we take for granted the help and support that others give to us in our times of need, but we should recognize that, in their presence, God is also present. His love and care for us become tangible and real in the concern and thoughtful gestures of others. This also means, of course, that we can be the means of making his presence real to others by responding to the promptings of the Spirit to express his love in practical ways.

I have been amazed myself at how often a word of encouragement has come to me just when I needed it. During a low point for me a few weeks ago, I said to God, 'Lord, I need some encouragement.' I didn't pray with any great fervour, but I did mean it. That same morning a letter came from a woman expressing her appreciation for my ministry and saying how much over the years she had been helped by the teaching seminars that I had led. This woman had no particular reason to write at that time, and she did not have my address, so she had clearly gone to some trouble to find it. That made her words all the more encouraging and real to me, for behind what she had written I could detect the voice of God, anticipating my need, reminding me of his presence.

Several of the individual words and phrases that David chooses here in Psalm 23 add to our encouragement. 'Even though'

> *Sometimes we take for granted the help and support that others give to us in our times of need*

reminds us that the valley experience is not what we should normally expect, but nevertheless, unusual as it is, it is not outside of God's control. Even in the extremes of Christian experience, God remains constant and faithful, and can be trusted.

'Even though I walk' teaches us that we do not have to run in blind panic when we meet adversity, but can trustingly walk by faith in every circumstance that confronts us. Walking is a common metaphor for the Christian life, and it suggests the measured pace of confidence in God rather than the frantic tizzy of unbelief.

'Even though I walk through' suggests that we will not be in the valley for ever. The experience will have an end, just as it had a beginning. As Julian of Norwich said, 'All things will pass', and the Shepherd who leads us into the valley will definitely lead us through it. We may wish to avoid it or skirt round it, but he will lead us through it. Darkness will give way to light; despair will yield to hope. We shall sing again.

'Even though I walk through the valley of the shadow' indicates that many of our fears are not grounded in reality. They are more imagination than truth. Most of our fears never materialize, they are merely shadows and have no real substance to them. Even death is but a shadow when seen in the light of Christ's triumphant resurrection. As Spurgeon said, the shadow of a dog cannot bite you, so why be afraid?

I have called this chapter 'The divine companion' because that is how David presents the Shep-herd to us. A companion is one who accompanies us, who shares the journey with us. Remember how God spoke to Moses? 'My Presence will go with you, and I will give you rest' (Exodus 33:14). It is a significant thought to grasp and bring into our thinking. God is with us. In grace he has chosen to share our journey. In grace he stoops down to be alongside us. We need not be afraid if he is our guardian and guide.

To order a copy of this book, please turn to page 159.

> *Even in the extremes of Christian experience, God remains constant and faithful*

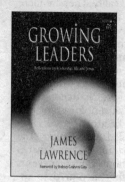

Recommended reading

Growing Leaders
by James Lawrence

In some church circles it is not unusual to be suspicious—not to say dismissive—of the application of 'business ideas' in what is deemed an exclusively 'spiritual' area—that of Christian leadership. After all, if the minister is sincere and prays a lot, surely s/he will manage their job without resorting to 'secular' jargon and techniques, as ministers have done down the centuries?

Growing Leaders paints a stark picture by way of an answer: seven out of ten Christian leaders today feel heavily overworked, four in ten suffer financial pressures, while only two in ten have had training in management or team building. A sobering total of 1,500 give up their job over a ten-year period. At the same time, as financial restrictions affect the availability of full-time ministers, more and more people are needed for leadership roles in local congregations, in every area of church work.

As well as presenting the bad news, though, *Growing Leaders* faces head-on the challenge of raising up new leaders and also helping existing leaders to develop and mature as they continue in their roles. It uses the model for growing leaders at the heart of the Arrow Leadership Programme, a ministry of the Church Pastoral Aid Society

(CPAS), which is managed by the book's author, James Lawrence.

James is an ordained minister in the Church of England and has spent time in parish ministry as well as being a member of Springboard, the Archbishops' initiative on evangelism. *Growing Leaders* is his second book for BRF: he has also written *Lost for Words* (BRF, 1999) and *Men: the Challenge of Change* (CPAS, 1997).

This new book reflects the breadth of his research into leadership and his ability to draw on an international range of sources. He also shares honestly some of his personal experiences—both positive and negative—in leadership situations, while noting the importance of acknowledging different personality types. What may work well for him could be the worst approach for somebody else.

One of the book's major themes

is how the key to fruitful leadership lies in awareness of the dangers of living in the 'red zone' of stress. James shows that, sadly, this is an all-too-common state of being for leaders, and he argues passionately for recognizing and then changing the factors that drive so many to burnout and even total breakdown. Instead of being driven by forces within ourselves that we have never admitted, let alone understood, we can learn to make wise choices and develop a rhythm of life that holds in balance work, leisure, friendship and family.

The book is clearly structured, with section headings that spell out the overall message: Growing leaders know they're chosen, discern God's call, develop Christ-like character, cultivate competence, and lead in community. A concluding resources section offers in-depth exploration of six themes mentioned more briefly elsewhere, from 'discerning your spiritual gifts' to 'guidelines for establishing a mentoring relationship'. Footnotes are sprinkled throughout the twelve main chapters, including books and websites for further study.

What impressed me most about *Growing Leaders*, however, is how it combines comprehensive analysis of good leadership skills with a stress on Christian discipleshipt. Building a close relationship with God is shown as central to true leadership competence, more foundational than the most insightful technique of secular management theory.

The book surveys relevant Bible passages to show how God can choose to call the most unlikely people to leadership, and that travelling the path of discipleship may involve discerning and then following that calling in obedience ourselves. Furthermore, those who are called to leadership are also called, to train up others as leaders. Some of the book's most thought-provoking sections argue for the crucial importance of team building, rather than the traditional 'lonely prophet on a mountain-top' leadership.

This is by no means a book for full-time ministers only. It is for anybody who exercises a leadership role (or who thinks they may be called to such a role) in either a church congregation or Christian organization. Another of the strengths of *Growing Leaders* is the way it demonstrates how many of the skills needed to lead a small Bible study group apply equally to leading a large team of co-workers in an office environment.

The awesome responsibility of leadership is summed up in the heading of the book's tenth chapter: 'Leaders discern, articulate and implement God's vision'. It both inspires leaders (and potential leaders) with the scope of their calling, while offering enough good advice and plain common sense to avoid any sense of being daunted by the task ahead.

Naomi Starkey, Commissioning Editor for BRF's Adult List.

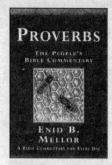

The People's Bible Commentary

One of the world's most famous books of wisdom, Proverbs is a collection of poems, wise sayings and short parables, showing how to apply godly principles to daily living. Some parts speak directly to young people, while others advise the leaders of the land. From first to last, however, we are reminded that the source of true wisdom is knowing God himself. The PBC volume on Proverbs is written by Enid B. Mellor, a former lecturer in religious education at King's College, London.

PROVERBS 8:12−21

The GIFTS *of* WISDOM

It may seem strange in our culture to have someone, however eminent and desirable, extol herself; in the ancient Near East it was not at all unusual for a deity to speak in praise of the gifts he, or sometimes, she, will give to her followers. The Canaanite god Baal says, 'I alone am he who will reign over the gods, yea, be leader of the gods and men.'

The ability to cope

Wisdom's associates are eminently desirable. She lives with prudence, and she is intimate with knowledge, discretion, insight, power and good advice (vv. 12, 14)—the things which in the first seven verses of Proverbs are set out as the basics of a moral and spiritual education, as essential to the wise as the Law is to the priest and the Word is to the prophet. They are all capacities which we need if we are to make sense of life and meet its demands, so we come back to the basic definition of Wisdom as 'the ability to cope'. They are human qualities which it is not beyond anyone to attain, but in the middle of describing them Wisdom points us to God (v. 13). Our moral and intellectual life should be inseparable from the spiritual, from our 'fear of the Lord'—our relationship of loving, reverent obedience with him

(1:7)—and from a hatred of everything that is arrogant, evil and crooked.

This echoes the description of the ideal king in Isaiah 11:2:

The spirit of the Lord shall rest on him, the spirit of wisdom and understanding, the spirit of counsel and might, the spirit of knowledge and the fear of the Lord.

Wisdom as a royal counsellor

Kings, rulers and nobles are mentioned elsewhere in Proverbs, and much of its advice is probably directed towards young men who are being trained for high office. On the whole, they are regarded favourably as people to be worked with, needing to be controlled by knowledge and discretion. Is human wisdom enough, or do they need divine Wisdom (vv. 15–16)?

The ideas in Proverbs should perhaps be taken together with those in the Psalms, where the king is often a person to be dealt with cautiously; it is God who is his guide and the source of his effectiveness as a ruler:

Give the king your justice, O God, and your righteousness to a king's son (Psalm 72:1).

Rewards

The rewards of following Wisdom at first look familiar: riches, good reputation, wealth and well-being (vv. 17–21; see 3:13–15). But they are not purely worldly benefits.

Justice and righteousness, that is, being right with God, will help to make and keep things right between people and between nations.

In verse 17 there is something else. Wisdom not only rewards those who follow her; she loves those who love her enough to persevere in their search for her. This is not a conditional promise; it is saying that we must earnestly desire Wisdom if we want to come into an intimate relationship with her, and that if we make this sincere effort, we can be sure of finding her.

To think about

How highly do I value Wisdom? What sacrifices will I make to be sure of finding her? What difference does she make to my life?

Prayer

Almighty God, the giver of wisdom, without whose help resolutions are vain, without whose blessing study is ineffectual; enable me, if it be thy will, to attain such knowledge as may qualify me to direct the doubtful and instruct the ignorant; to prevent wrongs and terminate contentions; and grant that I shall use that knowledge which I shall attain, to thy glory and my own salvation.
Samuel Johnson (1709–86)

To order a copy of this book, please turn to page 159.

For reflection

Confessions by Augustine of Hippo

'Great are you, O Lord, and greatly to be praised; great is your power, and infinite is your wisdom.' And man desires to praise you, for he is a part of your creation; he bears his mortality about with him and carries the evidence of his sin and the proof that you resist the proud. Still he desires to praise you, this man who is only a small part of your creation. You have prompted him, that he should delight to praise you, for you have made us for yourself and restless is our heart until it comes to rest in you.

Grant me, O Lord, to know and understand whether first to invoke you or to praise you; whether first to know you or call upon you. But who can invoke you, knowing you not? For he who knows you not may invoke you as another than you are. It may be that we should invoke you in order that we may come to know you. But 'how shall they call on him in whom they have not believed? Or how shall they believe without a preacher?' Now, 'they shall praise the Lord who seek him,' for 'those who seek shall find him,' and, finding him, shall praise him. I will seek you, O Lord, and call upon you. I call upon you, O Lord, in my faith which you have given me, which you have inspired in me through the humanity of your Son, and

> *When I call on him, I ask him to come into me*

through the ministry of your preacher.

And how shall I call upon my God—my God and my Lord? For when I call on him I ask him to come into me. And what place is there in me into which my God can come? How could God, the God who made both heaven and earth, come into me? Is there anything in me, O Lord my God, that can contain you? Do even the heaven and the earth, which you have made, and in which you did make me, contain you? Is it possible that, since without you nothing would be which does exist, you made it so that whatever exists has some capacity to receive you? Why, then, do I ask you to come into me, since I also am and could not be if you were not in me? For I am not, after all, in hell—and yet you are there too, for 'if I go down into hell, you are there'. Therefore I would not exist—I would simply not be at all—unless I exist in you, from whom and by whom and in whom all things are... Where, beyond heaven and earth, could I go that there my God might come to me—he who has said, 'I fill heaven and earth'?

Since, then, you fill the heaven and earth, do they contain you? Or, do you fill and overflow them, because they cannot contain you? And where do you pour out what remains of you after heaven and earth are full? ... the vessels which you fill do not confine you, since even if they were broken, you would not be poured out. And, when you are poured out on us, you are not thereby brought down; rather, we are uplifted. You are not scattered; rather, you gather us together. But when you fill all things, do you fill them with your whole being? Or, since not even all things together could contain you altogether, does any one thing contain a single part, and do all things contain that same part at the same time? Do singulars contain you singly? Do greater things contain more of you, and smaller things less? Or, is it not rather that you are wholly present everywhere, yet in such a way that nothing contains you wholly?

What, therefore, is my God? ... Most high, most excellent, most potent, most omnipotent; most merciful and most just; most secret and most truly present; most beautiful and most strong; stable, yet not supported; unchangeable, yet changing all things; never new, never old; making all things new, yet bringing old age upon the proud, and they know it not; always working, ever at rest; gathering, yet needing nothing; sustaining, pervading, and protecting; creating, nourishing, and developing; seeking, and yet possessing all things. You love, but without passion; are jealous, yet free from care; repent without remorse; angry, yet remaining serene. You change your ways, leaving your plans unchanged; you recover what you have never really lost. You are never in need but still you rejoice at your gains; are never greedy, yet demand dividends... Yet, O my God, my life, my holy Joy, what is this that I have said? What can any man say when he speaks of you? But woe to them that keep silence—since even those who say most are dumb.

Augustine of Hippo (345–430), From *Confessions*, Book 1, chapters 1—4

> *Since, then, you fill the heaven and earth, do they contain you?*

New Daylight © BRF 2004

The Bible Reading Fellowship
First Floor, Elsfield Hall, 15–17 Elsfield Way, Oxford OX2 8FG
ISBN 1 84101 304 8

Distributed in Australia by:
Willow Connection, PO Box 288, Brookvale, NSW 2100.
Tel: 02 9948 3957; Fax: 02 9948 8153;
E-mail: info@willowconnection.com.au
Available also from all good Christian bookshops in Australia.
For individual and group subscriptions in Australia:
Mrs Rosemary Morrall, PO Box W35, Wanniassa, ACT 2903.

Distributed in New Zealand by:
Scripture Union Wholesale, PO Box 760, Wellington
Tel: 04 385 0421; Fax: 04 384 3990; E-mail: suwholesale@clear.net.nz

Distributed in South Africa by:
Struik Book Distributors, PO Box 1144, Cape Town 8000
Tel: 021 462 4630; Fax: 021 461 3612; E-mail: enquiry@struik.co.za

Distributed in the USA by:
The Bible Reading Fellowship, PO Box 380, Winter Park,
Florida 32790-0380
Tel: 407 628 4330 or 800 749 4331; Fax: 407 647 2406;
E-mail: brf@biblereading.org; Website: www.biblereading.org

Publications distributed to more than 60 countries

Acknowledgments

Printed in Denmark

BRF seeks to help people of all ages to experience the living God—Father, Son and Holy Spirit—at a deeper level, and enable them to grow as disciples of Jesus Christ through the Bible, prayer and worship.

We need your help if we are to make a real impact on the local church and community. In an increasingly secular world people need even more help with their Bible reading, their prayer and their discipleship. We can do something about this, but our resources are limited. With your help, if we all do a little, together we can make a huge difference.

How can you help?

- You could become a *Friend of BRF* and encourage BRF's ministry within your own church and community (contact the BRF office, or visit the BRF website, www.brf.org.uk).

- You could support BRF's ministry with a donation or standing order (using the response form overleaf).

- You could consider making a bequest to BRF in your will, and so give lasting support to our work. (We have a leaflet available with more information about this, which can be requested using the form overleaf.)

- And, most important of all, you could become a BRF *Prayer Partner* and support BRF with your prayers. *Prayer Partners* receive our bimonthly prayer letter which includes details of all that is going on within BRF and specific prayer pointers for each prayer need. (To become a *Prayer Partner* write to BRF or e-mail enquiriesr@brf.org.uk)

Whatever you can do or give, we thank you for your support.

BRF MINISTRY APPEAL RESPONSE FORM

Name _____

Address _____

_____ Postcode _____

Telephone _____ Email _____

(tick as appropriate)

Gift Aid Declaration

☐ I am a UK taxpayer. I want BRF to treat as Gift Aid Donations all donations I make from 6 April 2000 until I notify you otherwise.

Signature _____ Date _____

☐ I would like to support BRF's ministry with a regular donation by standing order (please complete the Banker's Order below).

Standing Order – Banker's Order

To the Manager, Name of Bank/Building Society _____

Address _____

_____ Postcode _____

Sort Code _____ Account Name _____

Account No _____

Please pay Royal Bank of Scotland plc, London Drummonds Branch, 49 Charing Cross, London SW1A 2DX (Sort Code 16-00-38), for the account of BRF A/C No. 00774151

The sum of _____ pounds on ___ /___ /___ (insert date your standing order starts) and thereafter the same amount on the same day of each month until further notice.

Signature _____ Date _____

Single donation

☐ I enclose my cheque/credit card/Switch card details for a donation of £5 £10 £25 £50 £100 £250 (other) £ _____ to support BRF's ministry

Credit/ Switch card no. ☐☐☐☐☐☐☐☐☐☐☐☐☐☐☐☐☐☐☐☐

Expires ☐☐ ☐☐   Issue no. of Switch card ☐☐☐

Signature _____ Date _____

(Where appropriate, on receipt of your donation, we will send you a Gift Aid form)

☐ Please send me information about making a bequest to BRF in my will.

Please detach and send this completed form to: Richard Fisher, BRF, First Floor, Elsfield Hall, 15–17 Elsfield Way, Oxford OX2 8FG. BRF is a Registered Charity (No.233280)

ND0204

BIBLE READING RESOURCES PACK

A pack of resources and ideas to help to promote Bible reading in your church is available from BRF. The pack, which will be of use at any time during the year, includes sample editions of the notes, magazine articles, leaflets about BRF Bible reading resources and much more. Unless you specify the month in which you would like the pack sent, we will send it immediately on receipt of your order. We greatly appreciate your donations towards the cost of producing the pack (without them we would not be able to make the pack available) and we welcome your comments about the contents of the pack and your ideas for future ones.

This coupon should be sent to:

BRF
First Floor
Elsfield Hall
15–17 Elsfield Way
Oxford
OX2 8FG

Name —————————————————————————

Address ———————————————————————————

————————————————————————————————

————————————————————————— Postcode —————

Telephone —————————————————————————

Email —————————————————————————————

Please send me ————— Bible Reading Resources Pack(s)

Please send the pack now/ in ————————————— (month).

I enclose a donation for £ ————— towards the cost of the pack.

NEW DAYLIGHT SUBSCRIPTIONS

❏ I would like to give a gift subscription (please complete both name and
  address sections below)
❏ I would like to take out a subscription myself (complete name and
  address details only once)

This completed coupon should be sent with appropriate payment to BRF.
Alternatively, please write to us quoting your name, address, the subscription you
would like for either yourself or a friend (with their name and address), the start date
and credit card number, expiry date and signature if paying by credit card.

Gift subscription name _____

Gift subscription address_____

_____

_____Postcode _____

Please send beginning with the September 2004 / January / May 2005 issue:
(delete as applicable)

(please tick box)	UK	SURFACE	AIR MAIL
NEW DAYLIGHT	❏ £11.40	❏ £12.75	❏ £15.00
NEW DAYLIGHT 3-year sub	❏ £28.95		
NEW DAYLIGHT LARGE PRINT	❏ £16.80	❏ £20.40	❏ £24.90

Please complete the payment details below and send your coupon, with
appropriate payment to: **BRF, First Floor, Elsfield Hall, 15–17 Elsfield Way,
Oxford OX2 8FG.**

Your name _____

Your address_____

_____

_____Postcode _____

Total enclosed £ _____ (cheques should be made payable to 'BRF')

Payment by cheque ❏ postal order ❏ Visa ❏ Mastercard ❏ Switch ❏

Card number: ❏❏❏❏❏❏❏❏❏❏❏❏❏❏❏❏❏❏

Expiry date of card: ❏❏❏❏   Issue number (Switch): ❏❏❏❏

Signature (essential if paying by credit/Switch card)_____

❏ Please do not send me further information about BRF publications.

BRF is a Registered Charity

BRF PUBLICATIONS ORDER FORM

Please ensure that you complete and send off both sides of this order form.

	Please send me the following book(s):	Quantity	Price	Total
291 2	Song of the Shepherd (T. Horsfall)	____	£6.99	____
246 7	Growing Leaders (J. Lawrence)	____	£7.99	____
135 5	Easy Ways to Bible Fun for the Very Young (V. Howie)	____	£9.99	____
342 0	Easy Ways to Seasonal Fun for the Very Young (V. Howie)	____	£9.99	____
192 4	PBC: Leviticus and Numbers (M. Butterworth)	____	£7.99	____
095 2	PBC: Joshua and Judges (S. Mathewson)	____	£7.99	____
030 8	PBC: 1 & 2 Samuel (H. Mowvley)	____	£7.99	____
118 5	PBC: 1 & 2 Kings (S. Dawes)	____	£7.99	____
070 7	PBC: Chronicles—Nehemiah (M. Tunnicliffe)	____	£7.99	____
094 4	PBC: Job (K. Dell)	____	£7.99	____
031 6	PBC: Psalms 1—72 (D. Coggan)	____	£7.99	____
065 0	PBC: Psalms 73—150 (D. Coggan)	____	£7.99	____
071 5	PBC: Proverbs (E. Mellor)	____	£7.99	____
087 1	PBC: Jeremiah (R. Mason)	____	£7.99	____
040 5	PBC: Ezekiel (E. Lucas)	____	£7.99	____
028 6	PBC: Nahum—Malachi (G. Emmerson)	____	£7.99	____
191 6	PBC: Matthew (J. Proctor)	____	£7.99	____
046 4	PBC: Mark (D. France)	____	£7.99	____
027 8	PBC: Luke (H. Wansbrough)	____	£7.99	____
029 4	PBC: John (R.A. Burridge)	____	£7.99	____
082 0	PBC: Romans (J. Dunn)	____	£7.99	____
122 3	PBC: 1 Corinthians (J. Murphy-O'Connor)	____	£7.99	____
073 1	PBC: 2 Corinthians (A. Besançon Spencer)	____	£7.99	____
012 X	PBC: Galatians and 1 & 2 Thessalonians (J. Fenton)	____	£7.99	____
047 2	PBC: Ephesians—Colossians & Philemon (M. Maxwell)	____	£7.99	____
119 3	PBC: Timothy, Titus and Hebrews (D. France)	____	£7.99	____
092 8	PBC: James—Jude (F. Moloney)	____	£7.99	____

Total cost of books £ _____
Postage and packing (see over) £ _____
TOTAL £ _____

See over for payment details. All prices are correct at time of going to press, are subject to the prevailing rate of VAT and may be subject to change without prior warning.

The Bible Reading Fellowship is a Registered Charity

ND0204

Please complete the payment details below and send with appropriate payment and completed order form to:

**BRF, First Floor, Elsfield Hall,
15–17 Elsfield Way, Oxford OX2 8FG**

Name _____

Address _____

_____

_____ Postcode _____

Telephone _____

Email _____

Total enclosed £ _____ (cheques should be made payable to 'BRF')

Payment by cheque ❑ postal order ❑ Visa ❑ Mastercard ❑ Switch ❑

Card number: ⬚⬚⬚⬚⬚⬚⬚⬚⬚⬚⬚⬚⬚⬚⬚⬚⬚⬚⬚⬚

Expiry date of card: ⬚⬚⬚⬚   Issue number (Switch): ⬚⬚⬚⬚

Signature (essential if paying by credit/Switch card) _____

ALTERNATIVE WAYS TO ORDER

Christian bookshops: All good Christian bookshops stock BRF publications. For your nearest stockist, please contact BRF.

POSTAGE AND PACKING CHARGES				
order value	UK	Europe	Surface	Air Mail
£7.00 & under	£1.25	£3.00	£3.50	£5.50
£7.01–£30.00	£2.25	£5.50	£6.50	£10.00
Over £30.00	free	prices on request		

Telephone: The BRF office is open between 09.15 and 17.00.
To place your order, phone 01865 319700; fax 01865 319701.

Web: Visit www.brf.org.uk

❑ Please do not send me further information about BRF publications.

BRF is a Registered Charity